AU...A'S
TO.GHEST
PRISONS:
INMATES

AUSTRALIA'S TOUGHEST PRISONS:
INMATES

JAMES PHELPS

EBURY
PRESS

An Ebury Press book
Published by Penguin Random House Australia Pty Ltd
Level 3, 100 Pacific Highway, North Sydney NSW 2060
www.penguin.com.au

First published by Ebury Press in 2016
This edition published in 2017

National Library of Australia
Cataloguing-in-Publication entry

Phelps, James, author
Australia's toughest prisons: inmates/James Phelps

ISBN 978 0 14378 052 6

Prisoners – Australia
Prison violence – Australia
Prisons – Australia

Cover design by Luke Causby/Blue Cork
Cover photo © James Day/Getty Images
Internal design and typesetting by Midland Typesetters, Australia
Printed in Australia by Griffin Press, an accredited ISO AS/NZS 14001:2004
Environmental Management System printer

Penguin Random House Australia uses papers that are natural, renewable
and recyclable products and made from wood grown in sustainable forests.
The logging and manufacturing processes are expected to conform to the
environmental regulations of the country of origin.

Contents

The Inmate Code

DOG and die.

'Everyone knows you can't DOG [give information to police about another criminal],' said a man who spent more than half his life in jail for murder. 'This is the most important rule. But this isn't one of the rules you need to be told. It's a street rule and it's a prison rule. You never give anyone up. And if you do, then you will be got.'

GOT means dead.

'Got?' continued the former inmate. 'That means dead. On the street it could mean you're going to get bashed or whatever, but in prison it means you are going to get killed. If you hear word that someone is "after you", well, you better kill them before they kill you. There's no mucking around. People don't want to hurt you in prison. They want to *kill* you. You don't want to win a fight and then get shivved in the back the next week, month or year. You want to kill them so they don't ever get the chance.'

STICK to your own.

'It is forbidden to speak to someone from another race. In fact, in some jails you will get bashed by your own if you don't attack someone from another race when you get the chance. Polynesians and Asians stick together. They have their own wing in most jails. They are also allowed to stick with Aussies [Anglo-Saxons]. The Lebanese [men with Middle Eastern heritage] and the Aboriginals team up and have their own wings. There is a constant war between the two groups. It doesn't matter if a Lebo and a Poly were mates on the outside – on the inside they're enemies.'

KNOW the chain of command.

'You need to know who's in charge of your wing. And you need permission off them to do anything. There are stages and rankings in each race. There is a boss, then his right-hand man, and then it goes down the chain. You can't start something unless you have permission from the corporals, captains and lieutenants.'

DON'T ask for protection.

'You're a marked man if you ask to go into a protection wing. You are suspected of either being a DOG, a rock spider [paedophile] or someone who has committed crimes against women. Even if you haven't, if you are just weak and scared, you will be killed if anyone gets to you after you've asked for protection.'

Got all that? Good. Time to go inside. You'll be right . . . *I promise.*

1

INTRODUCING THE INMATES

Warning: the following material is sexually explicit and highly graphic.

Porky Pig

The 150kg pig sucked and slurped. His knees touching the cold concrete floor, he gulped and, occasionally, he gagged – the mass-murdering monster was unable to take the full thrust of what was being forced into his face.

Crack!

The cell door suddenly swung open.

'You fucking sicko!' the prison officer screamed, so disgusted he wanted to spew.

Martin Bryant spat out the penis. A little stunned – maybe even shocked – but certainly not sorry.

He didn't care . . . *as long as he got his chocolate.*

'I walked in on him once,' said the Risdon Prison officer who witnessed Australia's worst-ever killer sucking another inmate's penis in Tasmanian's most notorious jail.

'It's something I'll never forget, no matter how hard I try – Bryant giving a bloke a head-job in a cell. We knew he was a cat, who often performed sex acts on fellow inmates, but seeing was worse than knowing.'

Martin John Bryant, now almost 50, is a fat, bald sexual deviant dubbed 'Porky Pig'. He looks nothing like the pale, long-haired skeleton who killed 35 innocent people and injured another 23 in one of the world's worst shooting sprees. Bryant pulled out a Colt AR15 SPI semi-automatic and killed David and Sally Smith on 28 April 1996 before going on a rampage that would see 78 people shot in what became known as the 'Port Arthur Massacre'.

He now sucks cock for treats.

'He would perform sexual services for payment,' confirmed former senior Risdon corrections officer Tony Burley. 'I think it was mainly head-jobs, but he did other things too, I'm sure. He had plenty of opportunities to do it when he was locked away in the old prison hospital at Risdon. He'd be able to give a bloke a head-job in a yard, in a cell, in a laundry or at a toilet. He did it in most of those places.'

Bryant, an almost anonymous prisoner despite committing the crime that changed a young nation, spends his days sleeping and taking lonesome strolls around the yard.

Oh yeah . . . and doling out sexual favours.

'There's no doubt he's not right in the head,' said Burley, now retired. 'And the blokes who pay him for sex and head-jobs suffer from mental problems too. He was pretty infamous for these acts before the new prison was built and he was moved. We are talking from about 2000 to 2006.'

Bryant's preferred payment for prostituting himself was chocolate.

'He would do it for chocolate, or whatever else they had,' Burley continued. 'He loved chocolate.'

Bryant's weight fluctuates between 130 and 160kg, according to officers who guard the madman.

Maybe it depends on how much chocolate he can get his hands on?

'The officers called him Porky Pig on the account of his size,' Burley said. 'I reckon he gets a fair bit of chocolate.'

Sad. That's how Burley described Bryant's existence. 'He's the sort of bloke who doesn't really demand a lot of attention from the officers or raise too many alarms. He's fairly compliant and not considered dangerous. He would be at the bottom of the chain when it comes to dangerous prisoners or those who need observation and management.

'He has no hobbies and no jobs. He pretty much gets out of bed in the morning, wanders around by himself for a while, and then goes back to bed again.'

And he eats chocolate.

Bryant isn't the only sick, sad and disgusting sex fiend you are about to meet. Unfortunately, you will hear more about Bryant soon . . .

Gary Murphy, one of the men involved in the gruesome killing of Anita Cobby, might just be worse.

And he didn't even do it for chocolate . . .

'I was doing a few months at Parramatta back in the day,' a former inmate, who asked to remain anonymous, recalled. 'I was sent there for something quite minor – it might have been traffic offences. I would go back for much more serious things later.'

The fresh inmate saw an old friend shortly after he was received into the western Sydney jail.

'Hey, mate,' the friend had said. 'How you doing?'

'All good, mate,' the newbie replied. 'Only a short stay, so I can't complain.'

The established prisoner pointed towards a cell where a row of men were lined up like they were waiting for dinner. 'You want a suck? We have a cat down there giving all the boys head-jobs.'

The fine-avoider shook his head. 'I'm sweet. I'm only doing a few months. I'll be right.'

The older man was persistent. 'Nah, go on, mate,' he said. 'She'll be right. I'll get you straight to the front of the queue.'

Parramatta's newest inmate didn't want a 'suck'.

But the least he could do was go and have a look, right?

'Anyway, he opened the door and Gary Murphy was there,' the new inmate recalled. 'He was sucking one bloke off while another bloke was rooting him in the arse. I'd never seen anything like it before.'

4

'Why does he do it?' he asked the prison-hardened criminal, feeling sick. 'What's in it for him?'

'Nothing, mate. He's a jail cat. Go for it. Everyone roots him. He just likes it.'

There is no escaping the truth. Even though some might escape jail – and you will soon hear the first full account of the world's most famous jailbreak later – every prison in Australia is a house of horrors.

They are all bricks and bars, sex and stabbings, head-jobs and heroin. And in the following pages you'll read the full and shocking account of what jail is like, with some of Australia's most infamous inmates going on the record for the first time.

You will meet the alleged hitman and undisputed hardman called 'Goldie'; John Reginald Killick will divulge how he really escaped from Silverwater Jail in a helicopter and survived Pentridge Prison's 'Hell Block'; and former Rugby League star Craig Field will tell you his incredible story in a series of interviews conducted from inside a maximum-security jail.

But first, let's meet David Hooker . . . and find out how the juvenile justice system in New South Wales made him a murderer.

2

MAKING A MURDERER
Minda and Kariong

Uzzles

Flick. Nothing. *Flick.* Nothing. *Flick* . . . Finally the flint sparked the butane, sending the flame into the unfurled aluminum foil.

'Nah, not yet,' said the kid holding both the lighter and the sandwich wrapper he'd rescued from the bin. 'Wait. I'll tell ya when.'

The other kid – the one with the sipping straw stuck to his lip – pulled back. 'Yeah, sweet,' he said, nodding.

The flame turned the foil black, and the brown blob sitting on top began to bubble.

'Now,' said the cook. 'Rip in.'

Sitting on the concrete, a toilet the only thing between him and his newest mate, he leant in and sucked, aiming the end of the straw above the bubbling blob. He heaved into the smoke and inhaled with all his might.

'Hold it,' said the cook. 'Hold it in for as long as you can.'

So he did. Not daring to exhale until his face was red-raw from the strain.

Pfffffft.

Smoke spewed into the air as his lungs contracted explosively.

He waited.

Nothing.

'This ain't doing shit,' he coughed.

And then it came. The hit. The oblivion.

He smiled, not knowing he would soon be an addict . . . *A druggie at the age of 13.*

This is the shocking story of how a juvenile detention centre turned a child into a killer. How bashings, brawls and the ever-present badness of a house of horrors made a murderer.

And it all began with a spot of heroin, smuggled into the Minda Juvenile Justice Centre in south-west Sydney by a 16-year-old.

'I had a mate from school, and he was in there the same time as me,' said Dave Hooker, now 38, who bravely went on the record to tell his sad, sickening and soon-to-turn sinister story. 'He came up to me one day and asked me if I wanted some "uzzles". I didn't even know what the fuck it was. That was what they called H [heroin] in there. No idea why, but that's what they called it. I don't know how he got it, but he had it and I was up for anything.'

Hooker, a 13-year-old car thief and Minda's newest resident, nodded and said, 'Sure, why not?' Amid the monsters, most aged 18, more men than boys, sucking back on heroin was better than sitting alone and thinking about *when* – not *if* – he would be bashed for his shoes.

'He told me to meet him down by the toilets, so I did,' Hooker continued. 'He put the shit on the foil and gave me a straw and said, "Here you go." He sparked it up for me and I had a toke. I had a smoke afterwards while he was having a go. We went back and forth until it was all gone.'

The fear of being bashed, raped or just bloody bored was sucked from Hooker's body by the burning brown. Numb, the teenager walked out into the yard. He felt nothing . . . well, until he felt sick.

'I walked out into the yard and started spewing,' Hooker continued. 'I had been feeling smashed, awesome. There was nothing in my head. And then I started chucking all over the concrete. Blokes were looking at me like I was on fire or something. I was like, *What the fuck is this? What did I do that for?* I felt terrible.'

But there is no prize for guessing where this story goes. Like all soon-to-be addicts, he forgot about the chunks that had flown from his mouth and splattered onto the concrete floor, about the horrible headaches and the shakes he suffered throughout the night.

He went back for more, of course.

'I was around H all the time after that,' Hooker said. 'I would take it whenever it was around.'

So how does a 13-year-old get his hands on the world's most addictive, destructive drug while in a state-run juvenile centre? A place where he had been sent to 'learn his lesson', to reform and rehabilitate?

'It was easy to get in,' Hooker said. 'My mate was an Asian, and it was the other older Asian blokes who were giving it to him. I ended up meeting those older boys too, and they started giving it to me. I did it whenever I could get it. Sometimes it would be once a week. Sometimes it would be once every second day. It just depended how much was around and whose turn it was to get some.'

The infamous Sydney Vietnamese street gang called '5T', or the T's for short, were supplying heroin to the juvenile offenders, according to the kid who would become a teenage junkie.

5T was a murderous outfit that imported heroin from South-East Asia and flooded Sydney with the drug during the 1990s from their Cabramatta base.

'The T's were coming in and giving it to their younger brothers,' Hooker continued. 'The older boys would come in to visit and give it to them. It started becoming more regular from the time I got there, and eventually it was coming in every week.'

5T, cashed up from their roaring drug trade, handed the H over to their family members for free. They didn't know or care whether or not their brothers were taking the drug themselves or using it as currency.

'I never had to pay for it,' Hooker said. 'Not during my stint in Minda, anyway. I probably would have never become an addict if I wasn't getting it for nothing, because I *had* nothing. But in that place, at that time, we were all mates and we shared what we had. They were getting plenty, so they were happy to pass it around. It went that way until I got out.'

But this is where the story takes a darker turn – in Minda, with a 13-year-old sucking heroin through a straw next to a 'shitta', one night after being thrown in a cold, lonely cell, with nothing but a bed, a pillow and a blanket.

Huaraches

Hooker's highway to heroin had begun on a truck.

'Nice shoes, bro,' the Aboriginal boy, aged about 16, said. 'Nikes, hey? Yep, they'll be fuckin' mine by the end of the day.'

Hooker looked past the chains that connected the constricting cuffs and down to his Nike Huaraches planted on the bus floor.

He had bought 'the latest and greatest' in footwear not long before he stole a car and led police on a high-speed chase from Bankstown to Penrith. He'd used the money he'd stolen in an armed robbery to buy the $250 kicks.

'Yeah, we'll see about that,' Hooker replied.

The older kid, flanked by a posse of big boys who appeared to be his mates, smiled.

'Yep,' he fired. 'We sure will.'

Trying to be all tough and terrifying, Hooker stared at the mob as the truck rattled its way to Lidcombe – home of the Minda Juvenile Justice Centre.

'Obviously I was scared,' he recalled. 'You have that fear in ya – especially being just 13 – but I knew I couldn't be weak. I'd heard shit like this went on, and I was expecting it.

'I had already been printed and strip searched at the police station. I guess that's when you start getting a bit nervous. I was then transferred into a prison truck, and that is pretty shit. Once you get in the truck you're cuffed up and can't see shit. That was pretty bad.'

Then came the threat.

'There were a few Aboriginals on the truck, and I just thought, *Oh fuck*. You always hear about the Abos and how bad they are in jail. They want your shoes and all that sort of shit. They are pretty well known for sticking together in numbers and for cracking people.

'I thought, *Here we go. I'm about to have my first fight.* I had the latest Huaraches on at the time and thought, *No way are they getting these.*

And, yep . . . they tried it on.

The taunts and threats went back and forth until the bus stopped at Minda – the 'junior jail' that has housed the worst juvenile offenders in New South Wales since 1966. No doubt some of them were now buried in nearby Rookwood Cemetery – the famous graveyard a frightfully fitting neighbor for this living hell.

'When I got out of the truck, they handcuffed me to one of the Abos who wanted my shoes,' Hooker said. 'They split us into groups of two so they could do the searches, and that's when you start to feel really vulnerable.'

Hooker wasn't just worried about copping a hiding from

the older, stronger kid linked to him by the cold chain. No . . . He was even more terrified of the guards and their *plastic latex gloves*.

'Get 'em off,' the officer said. 'Everything. Take every item of clothing off right now, including your socks and shoes.'

Not so bad, Hooker initially thought. *Same as the cop shop.*

'But then he screamed at me to bend over,' Hooker said, recalling the horrifying experience. 'And he went right on with it, looking in my arse, grabbing at my balls. It was fucking terrible, only being a kid. And I don't think they were just searching us for gear . . . I think it was a bit of a scare tactic as well.'

And it worked.

'I remember walking into the main jail after being searched, and everything just became narrow,' he said. 'It was like I had tunnel vision. I kept my eyes down and looked at nothing. And I said nothing until they screamed my name. That was a reality check too, because no one called me by my name. I hadn't heard my own name for a while, because on the streets I had my street name. A nickname.'

The reception guard fired off a full magazine lode of questions: *What's your date of birth? Do you have any gang affiliations? Do you have any tattoos? Are any of your co-offenders incarcerated here? Do you have any enemies that might be here?*

'I remember looking into a wing while he was asking me shit,' Hooker continued.

'And I could see all these perspex windows. Behind them I could see all these blokes. They were yelling out, screaming and banging on the glass.'

Yep. Now he was scared. Shitting bricks.

'The boys in there were aged anywhere from ten to 18,' Hooker said. 'But when I walked in, all the guys I'd first seen were 17, so to me they were men. I was still a little kid and they were all developed and quite big. I remember looking at the Islander boys – they were just fucking huge. I started worrying then. I was sure I was going to have to fight them.'

A guard screamed his name: 'David Hooker!' The name he hadn't heard since the day he'd quit school. *Primary school.*

'He handed me a pile of clothes,' Hooker said. 'They were all black. Others guys had been given other colours, and I wondered what it was all about. It was a colour code. Whatever colour they gave you determined where you went. Black meant I was going to a wing called Kendall.'

The rest of the new inmates were given different colours and sent off to four other wings: McKellar, Transit, Talbot or Lawson.

'Hookzy!' a boy screamed as he entered the wing. 'What the fuck are you doing here?'

The familiar face forced out the fear.

'I was relieved straightaway because all these blokes I grew up with on the street were there,' Hooker said. 'I can't remember how many, but there were a few, and right then and there I knew I'd be sweet. They were older than me, and tough too. You have all your little groups and gangs in Minda. And when I got put in, most of the blokes were from Bankstown, which is where I'm from. It was the closest jail to Bankstown, so that's where all the boys from round there went.'

Maybe this won't be so bad? Hooker thought. *Maybe I won't be killed after all?*

'The boys pulled me aside and told me it was still a fucking madhouse,' Hooker said. 'They told me you get fucked up big-time if you didn't follow the rules.'

Then they gave him the prison code – the unwritten laws that might just save his life. *Or end it . . .*

'They told me what not to do and what I should be doing,' Hooker said. 'First up, they told me everything in jail was political. They said there are the blacks, there are the whites, there are the Asians, there are the Islanders, and there are the Lebos.

'They also told me some of the guys were linked to some pretty big street gangs, like 5T and all that kind of shit.'

Hooker stood with his mates and they looked around the wing. One pointed. 'See him?'

Hookz nodded.

'Don't fuck with him. And see that bloke?'

Hookz nodded again.

'5T.'

'They told me who the big people were and who I shouldn't take on,' Hooker recalled of the briefing. 'They also told me not to give anyone up, and I was just like, *Shit, I know that. That's a street rule.* The rest of it was pretty simple. They basically said stick with us and you'll be sweet. They said keep to yourself when you aren't with us, and don't fuck with anyone we've pointed out. And if anything goes wrong, we'll sort it out. Shit like that.

'I didn't think anything of it back then – it all seemed like a bit of fun – but looking back now it was pretty hectic. We were just kids, but we were already into prison codes. Blood in, blood out – you know?'

But for now he didn't care. All that mattered was that he had his boys, had his Huaraches. Everything would be sweet.

Or so he thought . . .

Bashed, Broken and a Bum Full of Tobacco

'Where the fuck is it, *Hooker*?' yelled the guard, spit spraying as he screamed at the kid.

He had unlocked the heavy metal door and launched into the cell – a 4 metre by 3 metre concrete room.

'Where is what?' Hooker replied as he sprang to attention. 'I ain't got shit, sir.'

The guard looked around. It was difficult to hide anything in a place like this. Scarily similar to any cell in an adult jail, light came in through a small barred window covered in perspex peppered with breeze holes. The door was solid steel with an 'observation window' cut into the middle.

The fresh inmate only had a bed, a toilet and a small shelf to keep his belongings . . . but it was bare. The only thing Hooker owned in Minda was now between his arse cheeks . . .

'Someone had slid me a ciggie under the door,' Hooker recalled. 'We used to tie shit to cotton and push it across the floor and under the door with a stick or something. On this occasion the officer actually saw it being dragged across the floor. He came in to have a go at me and I told him I didn't have shit. I told him to prove it, but he couldn't find it because I had it in my arse cheeks. In my "safe" . . . *ha*. That's what we called it.'

'Bullshit,' the guard had said. 'I saw you pull something under the door.'

Hooker shook his head, a giant smirk plastered on his face. Soon the officer had a companion. Another burly beast barged into the room and stood just in front of the open door.

'Bend over, you little shit,' said the accuser. 'Drop your dacks, cunt, and spread your cheeks.'

Oh no.

'Fuck off, you faggot,' Hooker said defiantly. He pointed at the officer guarding the door. 'Go look in your mate's arse if that's your thing.'

Whoosh!

The guard grabbed the boy – all 45kg of him – and threw him across the room.

Bang!

Hooker's tiny frame slammed into the wall, all brick and concrete render.

The guard who'd tossed him rushed forward, as did the other loitering guard.

They both grabbed the kid before hoisting him, with only the slightest effort, two feet into the air. And then they shook him – *up, down, left, right.* Hookzy was a ragdoll whose stitches stretched as he was swung, slapped and eventually dropped on his head.

'They came over and threw me around,' Hooker said. 'They were trying to make [the tobacco] drop, but I was clenching my arse for the life of me to keep it in there.'

His pants had been ripped off. He was all arse, balls and swinging cock. They shook harder.

Whack!

'I cracked one of them in the mouth,' Hooker continued. 'I wasn't about to take that shit. I didn't really care about being caught with the gear, but to be hurled around in the nude by two faggots was just humiliating.'

The officer reeled, surprised by the force of the blow.

Can a 13-year-old really hit that hard?

He didn't stop to consider his question before returning payment – with interest, of course.

'He didn't like it when I hit him,' Hooker said. 'He was a big unit, probably about 110kg. And he flogged the shit out of me.'

Umphhh! Umphhh!

It started with two body blows, but Hooker was punched in the face after he hit the officer again.

'Once I started throwing, the other bloke came in too. They gave me a hiding, smashing my face in before putting me in a headlock, trying to choke me out.'

And boy, did it hurt.

'I was a mess. I was sent to the hospital with "self-inflicted injuries". *Ha!* I had bruises everywhere – my arms, legs, even footprints on the side of my ribs. You could see the shoe marks from where they had stomped me with their boots. My whole neck was bruised from the strangling they gave me.'

His face, too, was swollen and covered in blood.

What did the nurse do, aside from treat his wounds? *Nothing.*

'I couldn't say anything,' Hooker recalled of the incident. 'I just had to cop it. I couldn't dob, and no one who worked there put the screws in.'

The only thing Hooker could do was issue a threat of his own. As the instigating officer dragged him from the floor, the belted, bruised and busted kid made a bold threat. A brave promise considering he could have been flogged – there and then – again.

'I told him I was going to upend him the next time he opened the door. I told him he wouldn't see it coming.'

The officer laughed . . .

Sadly, at Minda (and, to be fair, other juvenile detention institutions around Australia) bashings were common. Another former 'juvie' confirmed the brutality of the junior jails.

'The guards would come in and give you a flogging,' said the reformed 42-year-old, who asked not to be named. 'Some of them would just throw you around . . . or that's how it would start, anyway. It would be verbal at first. They would say, "Shut the fuck up or we'll come in and smash you."

'And us, being the rowdy little fuckers we were, would say, "Yeah, come in. Bring it on." They would then open up the door. Four of them would come in. Two would give you the hiding, one would be at the door, and one would be in the corridor. The guy in the hall would just be shutting everyone else up, and the one at the door would stop anyone else from getting in.

'They'd throw you around and it would just egg us on. We would start throwing punches and they would throw them back.'

He recalled one particular bashing he'd received in Minda.

His crime? *Talking.*

'They said they were going to give me a hiding one day because I was talking too much. I told them to fuck off – I would talk whenever I wanted.'

He got belted, *of course.*

As for Hooker and his brave threat? The 13-year-old and his promise to 'upend' the guard who'd left him black and blue but failed to find the tobacco stuffed in his arse?

'He eventually came back to my cell,' Hooker said. 'And, yep . . . I got him.'

His revenge did not come swiftly, but it did come – with a thunderous crack to the face.

'I waited a while so I could build up a few points for good behaviour,' Hooker continued. 'When you had enough points they gave you things, like books and maybe a TV. I ended up with a radio. It had three of those big D batteries in it. So I put them in a sock.'

He waited, waited and waited some more. Eventually Mr 'Drop-Your-Dacks-Cunt' entered his cell. And he copped a half-kilo cannonball to the face.

'He came through the door and I swung it at him. I think I broke his jaw.'

Segregation

Hooker copped another belting for breaking the guard's jaw with the loaded sock.

Is that your best? Another flogging? Big deal. Is that the worst you can do to me?

It wasn't. He was about to learn that there were worse things than bruises and broken bones: 'They put me in a segregation cell.'

Crack!

The door slammed and he was alone. A 120-watt globe flooded the concrete cell with blinding white light. No bed or blankets. No cupboards or shelves. There wasn't even a window. Just hard concrete flooded by a sea of unrelenting, blinding light.

'I didn't think it was too bad at first,' Hooker said. 'I knew about segro and knew others who had been thrown in there too. I'd heard the stories and they weren't all that bad. It was uncomfortable and shit, and the food they gave you was terrible, but by law they could only lock you in for 12 hours.'

Twelve hours on a cold concrete floor? *Piece of piss.*

'Or that's what I thought,' Hooker continued.

Seven hundred and twenty minutes later – 12 hours to the very second – the door opened.

'Let's go, *HOOKER*!' the officer boomed, flanked by his obliging buddy. 'You're out of here.'

Yep. Piece of piss. Over and out.

'But they walked me past my wing,' Hooker said. 'And that's when I started getting worried.'

Worried? No, he should have been *terrified*. And he would have been, had he known the officers at Minda Juvenile Justice Centre were about to exploit the system – and break the law – by stuffing the now 14-year-old in solitary confinement for a week.

'The pricks put me in for the 12 hours,' Hooker explained, 'but then they transferred me to another wing and put me in a different segro cell for *another* 12 hours. I went back and forth like that for a week. It was illegal, but if anyone looked at the cameras they would have gotten away with it because I was only spending 12 hours in any one cell.'

Yep, 12 hours was a piece of piss, but how about 168 hours? Or 10,080 minutes?

'The segro cells at Minda never had beds in them because they were designed to be used for just 12 hours,' Hooker continued. 'There was no need for anyone to sleep. So, yeah, it was fucked. All I did for a week was sit on a concrete floor and eat shit food. My back was so fucked. It seized up after a day or so.'

And, to make things worse . . . it was the middle of winter.

'It was fucking freezing, so I couldn't even use my shirt as a pillow because it was too cold. I got to sleep for about half an hour at a time – and that was it.'

Five days into his sleepless nightmare he decided he would go on a hunger strike.

'I refused to eat and they ended up letting me out two days later,' Hoooker said. 'I reckon they would have kept me in there if they weren't worried about me starving to death.'

So he went back to Kendall Wing . . . and back to the boredom that forced him to foil, flames and the bubbling brown.

Butts and Boredom

He stood and watched the guard suck back on his cigarette. So did four other boys, all out in the yard after finishing lunch – fish cocktails on this day. They all waited and watched.

Any moment now. He's almost done.

The guard exhaled, sending a final puff of smoke into the sky, and flicked his butt.

Again they waited, this time for the guard to walk away. And then the race was on – all five boys rushing towards the smouldering remains of the cigarette as the guard moved to another section of the yard.

'We would race over and grab [the cigarette butts] as soon as they dropped them,' Hooker said. 'All the screws smoked, and they would be walking around, flicking their butts all over the place. We'd collect them and find paper and shit to make Tally-hos, and then we'd make smokes.'

The boys would wait until 3pm before lighting up.

'The only reason we did it was to stop the boredom after lockdown,' he continued. 'We had to do shit like that to entertain ourselves. We would smoke in our cells, just for something to do.'

Lighters?

'No,' Hooker said. 'But we'd eventually work out a solution for anything. We'd rig up the power outlet with some steel wool or something to make a spark. And then we would smoke all night.'

That is . . . if you'd collected enough butts during the day.

'You would sing if you couldn't smoke,' Hooker said. 'That's about all you could do.'

A draconian reward and punishment system meant that most boys spent 15 hours a day locked in their cells with no TVs, no radios and no books.

'They would shut you in your cell at 3pm on the dot, no exceptions,' Hooker said. 'All you had was yourself and your bed for most of the time. Televisions and books were for the kids who behaved the best.

'You got ratings on things, and those with the highest scores got the rewards. They would check your cell in the morning to see if you had made your bed and rate you from one to five. You would get a five for a good-looking bed. There were points for other stuff too, and the person with the most points at the end of the month would be rewarded with a radio for a month, or a book for a month.'

But these reward items were limited: one TV up for grabs in his wing, two radios, two Walkman cassette players and a book.

Yep . . . one book.

'There was a library in the jail,' Hooker said, 'but you couldn't take the books out. You could only read them in the library.'

Minda was worse than Goulburn's Supermax, which holds monsters like Ivan Milat, when it came to privileges. Even the Backpacker Murderer gets books, a TV and even his own kitchen – complete with a microwave and a toaster (at least when he's not lopping off his fingers or burning down his cell).

The boredom was too much for some boys.

'A lot of kids killed themselves,' said another former

Minda detainee. 'And I reckon most had a go at some point. The nights just sucked. You would try not to go to sleep too early, because if you went to sleep at 4 or 5pm, then you'd wake up at 1am. And trust me, that was shit. So you'd stay up for as long as you could. You would try and yell out to boys across the wing and talk shit. That's all we had to do.

'The screws would tell us to shut up, and all that shit. And they would give us a hiding sometimes if we didn't shut up. But it didn't stop us. Boredom would take over and you would risk a hiding just to beat the boredom.

'Even being bashed was better than being bored.'

Things weren't much better when the sun rose, their 15-hour hell ending with the turn of a key.

'The doors would open and we had to shower,' he continued. 'It was two at a time and there were cubicles, so nothing really ever happened in the showers. Not like the stuff you see in movies.'

Then it was off to breakfast – a bowl of cereal, a sachet of sugar and a 250ml carton of milk.

'Then we got put into the yard. Every wing had its own yard, and there was also a main yard. There was a big oval and every department could use it but at different times. Every hour they would swap wings and you would get your turn to go and have a game of footy or whatever. That was the only thing I looked forward to.'

Others had nothing to look forward to. Many were terrified of being belted by the bigger, tougher boys.

'You couldn't go back and lock yourself in your cell if you were scared,' the former Minda juvie said. 'There was no protection. The only protection you could get was standing next to the guard supervising the yard. There was no boneyard [protection yard for Dogs], nothing like they have in the big jails.'

It was easy for a hunter to pick their prey.

'Oh, the weak ones,' he continued. 'Yeah, they were always standing near the officers.'

The tough ones?

'*Ha!* They were standing as far away from them as they could, hiding round corners and getting up to shit.'

No one was immune from a beating in Minda. Sure, the weak ones – those who stuck to the guards like remoras to sharks – copped it the worst. Unlike the tiny feeding fish, they were easily shaken by their hosts. Even the big boys blued, violence another way to beat the boredom.

'There were always fights,' Hooker recalled. 'I had a couple . . . We all did. They would start because of bullshit. People would gee you up. They would come over and say that some bloke called you a dickhead. You would then go over and start a fight.'

Later, the brawling boys would find out that nothing had actually been said: *What? I started him for nothing? He didn't call me a dickhead?*

'The other guys would just make it up because they wanted to see a fight,' Hooker said. 'It was something for them to do, some excitement. They were just trying to entertain themselves. I had a go at one bloke, and as we were having a dig I could hear people laughing in the background because it was a gee-up.'

Boys setting up fights? Nothing unusual about that, you might say. It happens in every schoolyard across Australia. But in Minda, the boys knew how to fight.

They also knew how to kick, stomp, bite and stab. *And sometimes they killed . . .*

'The kids could do some massive damage,' Hooker recalled. 'They were fucking crazy. They had no real form. It was more just swinging as hard as you could.'

The junior criminals were ruthless.

'They would stomp on your head if they got you on the ground. Noses and jaws were always broken. They also stabbed each other with shivs. I was a fighter and could handle myself. I got brought up boxing. You have to know how to handle yourself if you end up in any jail. It doesn't matter how quiet you keep, you will get picked eventually . . . especially in juvie. It's fight or die. You can't hide forever, and even being the best fighter in the world won't save you . . . not when you get stabbed in the back with a shiv.'

Lunch was served between fighting and footy.

'We got sandwiches. Ham, cheese and salad. It wasn't bad. We would eat it in the dining room before going back out to the yard.'

And then came lockdown . . . 3pm. *Lights out.*

Kariong
'Fuck this!' he screamed. 'I'm over it. I'm goin' to kill one of these cunts!'

27

Hooker, the 13-year-old first-time offender now a 17-year-old heroin addict and convicted armed robber, smiled and nodded. 'Fuck yeah, bro. Do it. Go on then.'

So the other inmate did, approaching the first officer he saw – a big man with his back turned.

Crack!

The guard, a senior officer at the Kariong Correctional Centre on New South Wales's Central Coast, was smashed in the back of the head. All hook, swing and fist hitting temple, the boy downed the guard with a dog shot. Guard on the ground, the kid pulled a knife from his pants and slashed at the punch-drunk officer's face.

Blood spurted from the wound, hitting his attacker, the wall and the ground. But before the free-flowing claret had time to pool on the concrete – *and it would* – the boy dropped behind the guard and joined him on the floor. He locked his legs around the concussed man's waist, pinning the guard to the ground. Then he placed his victim in a one-arm headlock. With the other hand, he held the blade to the fallen officer's throat.

'I'm going to cut your throat, cunt,' he said.

And so began a two-hour siege with a bleeding guard held hostage and a 15-year-old kid, who just wanted a smoke, ready to kill.

'We'd had haircuts the day before,' Hooker said. 'A lady came in once a month. My mate had stolen her mirror and shoved it down his pants.'

The 15-year-old – with fresh short back and sides – took the mirror back to his cell and smashed it, turning the vanity device into razor-sharp shards, each piece a potential murder weapon.

'He already had a table tennis paddle in his cell,' Hooker said. 'He broke the top off so it was just a handle.'

Hooker's mate selected the longest, thickest and most jagged shard and jammed it into the handle. He then bound it with shampoo bottle stickers he had stashed in his cell after a month of sneaking them from the showers.

'He told me he wanted to get a guard because he was just sick of all the shit that went on in [Kariong],' Hooker continued. 'I mean, plenty of shit went on, but it was cigarettes that tipped him over the edge. He wanted a cigarette and nobody had any, and it just set him off.

'He said he was sick of being treated like a kid and wanted to fuck up an officer so he could go to a real jail and be treated like a man.'

Yep . . . He was ready to kill a guard so he could be sent to a place where he could smoke. He was prepared to sacrifice up to 25 years of his life – locked up with other murderous men, the likes of the Cobby Killers, triple-murderer Michael Kanaan and maybe even Ivan Milat – for the right to own a packet of cigarettes.

'He went off his tree and I egged him on,' Hooker said. 'I was a fucking dickhead back then. I just told him to do it.'

And do it he did.

'He walked up to this screw and gave him a big crack across the head. He then sat him down and put the blade to his throat.'

Then he issued his demand.

'Get me a smoke, you cunts!' he screamed as every officer on duty stormed the wing. 'Do it or he's dead.'

The kid pressed the blade into the guard's neck, forcing the red welt to seep blood.

'The officer was shitting himself,' Hooker continued. 'I could see the fear in his eyes. He was terrified. I will never forget the look on his face. [The hostage-taker] kept on threatening to put it through his throat until he got a smoke.'

Kariong's Governor was now in the room. 'For Christ's sake!' he screamed, taking command. 'Get the kid a smoke.'

The officers shrugged in unison.

'I don't smoke,' said one.

'I'm out,' said another.

'I've got one!' someone yelled from a cell. 'I'll slip it through the door as long as I don't get charged.'

The 'Guv' agreed. 'Open that cell,' he ordered, pointing at a guard. 'Get the smoke. NOW.'

It was too late . . .

The nicotine-crazed kid shoved the shiv into the officer's throat while the screw was putting the key in the door.

'He jammed it in about two inches,' Hooker said. 'Blood started spurting everywhere. It was a fucking mess.'

The guards – stunned, shocked and fucking mad – stormed towards the boy and their bleeding colleague.

'Keep back or I'll kill him!' the kid screamed as he began twisting the shiv, turning flesh into mince.

'The bloke was dying,' Hooker said. 'He was going to bleed to death. I couldn't watch on as this bloke died, so I asked the screws to let me out of my cell. I promised I could talk him down. He was twisting the knife and making a mess. It was horrible to watch and I felt for the guard. I didn't want him to die. No one deserves that for doing their job. So I promised I could talk him down.'

And Hooker did.

'They let me out and I told him to let the guard go. I said, "It's not worth it," and I handed him a smoke.'

And the kid got his wish.

'They sent him to Silverwater,' Hooker said. 'But he was kept in segregation for two-and-a-half years until he turned 18.'

As for our 13-year-old junkie who became the 17-year-old criminal who saved the officer's life?

'I got out of juvie,' Hooker said, 'and I joined up with a bad crew. I was a fully blown addict and I ran drugs in the Cross. Eventually I was convicted of murder, robbery in company, and assaults too. I was 17 when I stabbed a bloke to death.'

Hooker would be convicted of the murder and incarcerated until he was in his mid-30s. He now has a young family and lives well away from his old stomping ground.

He has genuinely turned his back on crime. He is one of the rare reformed, and somebody this author is happy to call a friend.

So did the New South Wales Juvenile Justice system create this murderer? Did Minda and Kariong turn this one-time car thief into a killer?

Hooker, who now runs a successful and, more importantly, *legitimate* business, is reflective. 'That's difficult to say . . . Look, I was always going to be a criminal of some sort. I couldn't escape that because of my upbringing. I grew up in a family of crims, and I grew up really quickly because I wanted to be like them. I wanted to be in the game, just like them.

'I suppose my life was chosen for me. I was real young but I would still pick up on things that were happening in the house. I grew up in a house with 12 people. My uncle was one of Sydney's biggest car thieves, and the rest were into all sorts of crimes.

'Everyone at home was always talking about crime-related matters. About court appearances and bailing people out. About who got away with what and how much money they were making, or how much they'd been ripped off. I was learning about crime from a very young age. It was put in my head without me having a choice or knowing it.'

The car thief was Hooker's role model, his mistaken hero.

'I really looked up to my uncle. He was a great person on one front, but on the other he was a crim. I thought he was the best and I wanted to be like him. He was a nice bloke and he was making money. I wanted to be a nice bloke who made money too. You follow that path. It's tragic, but that's the way it goes.'

But heroin? *Murder?*

'Well, they never did anything like that,' Hooker continued. 'I became addicted to heroin while in juvie. I don't think that would have happened if I hadn't been put through the system. And my murder, my major crimes were a result of me being an addict.'

So did juvie make you a criminal?

'No.'

Did juvie make you a junkie?

'Yes.'

And did juvie make you a murderer?

'I would have to say it did. Or at the very least, the system has to cop some of the blame.'

It's hard to argue. He was given no education, was continually belted by guards and became a heroin addict in a public institution.

Now, let's find out where murderers go after they are made . . .

3

RECEPTION, RACE AND RAPE
Silverwater

Reception

The gavel came down.

'Bail is refused,' said the magistrate. 'You have been charged with the crime of murder in the first degree. You will be held in custody at the Metropolitan Remand and Reception Centre [MRRC] at Silverwater until you face trial. Given your record and your alleged crime, you pose a considerable risk to the safety of others.'

The 24-year-old was cuffed and thrown onto a prison bus. He was about to spend his first night in a maximum-security jail.

'I was actually pretty drug-fucked when I got on the bus,' recalled the inmate, who would eventually be convicted of murder and sentenced to serve a maximum of 21 years.

'I smoked a shitload of weed and whatever before I went to court. I knew I wasn't getting bail, so I got as wasted as I could. I can't tell you much about the bus ride. I don't think I was worried . . . only because I was too fucked up to be thinking at all.'

Silverwater would soon smash him sober. He started shitting himself the moment he was shoved into a cell.

'There were about 20 or so others in there with me,' he said of Silverwater's latest intake. 'They were all waiting to go to reception. I got in there, and they asked me if I was bikie and all that sort of shit before giving me a MIN number [Master Index Number – six digits an inmate will keep for life].

'They asked me if I was going to neck up [commit suicide], if I had enemies and if I wanted to be put in protection. It was fucking scary in that cell. All these big men with tatted-up faces and shit were just staring at me. They were mean-looking fuckers. There was another couple of blokes on the nod . . . junkies who were on the methadone or whatever.'

The new resident looked around, never staring . . . He didn't want a fight, but he snuck a quick peek at the men with the tattoos, the junkies and the others who just stared at the floor.

'I started noticing the race thing right there and then,' he said. 'I had heard about it, but I didn't really think about it too much or know what to expect.'

But it had already begun as he stood there in the reception cell.

'The Aussies were standing with Aussies,' he continued,

'the blacks with blacks, and the Lebos were in another corner, keeping to themselves. There was a lot of tension in there. I was sort of standing by myself, thinking, *What the fuck is going on here?* I'm an Islander but I could be mistaken for an Aussie, a Lebo, or even an Asian. I look like a bit of a mix.

'I didn't know what to do, and I thought it was going to bust up and go off. I wanted to go over near the Islanders but was too worried in case they figured I was a Lebo or something and belted me. I was on my own and felt very vulnerable. If a fight started – and I thought it would – I was going to have to fight them all.'

Then came the screams.

'Arrrrgh! Arrrrgh!'

Then more.

'Arrrrgh! Fuck you!'

'A couple of blokes were going off,' he said. 'We could hear them coming down the hall. I couldn't see out of the cell but it sounded like some crazy shit.'

The weed – and 'whatever else' – had worn off. He was now completely sober and scared.

'I just thought, *How am I going to get through this?*"

The door swung outwards and a screw sung out his name.

'He called me and this Aussie fella out, and they put us into a smaller cell.'

Thank fuck.

'I was glad to be out of that cell with all those blokes, but I had no idea why we'd been pulled out. I started to worry again.'

But this was nothing sinister.

'The officer said, "You two are going to Darcy," referring to a wing at the MRRC. I didn't know what the fuck that was.'

But he would soon find out.

'He led us out and Darcy was actually the first area you walk into. The first wings in the jail were called Darcy 1 and Darcy 2. We walked in and were issued with gear.'

Yep . . . the Aussie and the ambiguous-looking 24-year-old who was in fact an Islander were each given a green jumpsuit, a plastic bowl, a plastic mug, toothpaste, a toothbrush, a towel, a blanket and a pair of shoes with velcro fasteners.

'Yeah, no laces,' the former inmate recalled. 'You can neck yourself with them – *ha!* After they gave me my gear I was led down a big hall. And that's when reality hit. I thought, *Oh shit.*'

The reception was fronted by safe cells – all perspex, 24-hour cameras and filled with complete and utter crazies.

'I'd heard the stories about max, and here I was. But nothing could have prepared me for this. It didn't really look like a prison – not like you would expect. It felt more like a hospital. There was a long corridor that had doors every couple of metres. It was clean, sterile and had a really strange smell. Kind of like shit covered with clean. Each door led to a wing. They took me through the second one and shoved me in a little cage.

'They took the cuffs off and let me just stand there and look around. I could see into the wing and at this time it was in lockdown. All the boys were in their cells and it was quiet, hardly a sound.

'They opened up the gate and brought me in. An officer led me towards a cell. I heard this screaming and looked around. All the bottom cells were completely see-through and this naked bloke was going off. He was smashing his cock into the perspex door.'

Penis into perspex?

'Yep,' he continued. 'He was an absolute nutter and was going off his tree. Absolutely ape-shit. He was trying to tear his cock apart. I was fucking terrified.'

What is this place? A fucking circus? The lowest circle of hell?

'They went in and suited him up like Hannibal Lecter. They gagged his mouth and all of that. I found out later that blokes like him are called "spinners". That means they're fucking nuts.'

Okay, show's over. Time to see your 'new home'.

Cellmate No.1

The officer cracked the cell.

'This is you,' he said, waving him into the unknown.

Bang!

And with that the door was shut.

Welcome to 'Hotel Silverwater'.

'There was a Lebanese guy sitting on one of the two beds,' the former MRRC inmate said. 'And I just thought, *Fucking hell. How's this going to turn out?* I'd heard about all the race stuff and saw a bit of it earlier with the tension in the holding cell. And here I was . . . an Islander stuck with a Leb.'

Shit. What do I do?

Slowly, silently, he edged his way into the cell, staring at nothing but floor and wall. He put his prison-issued kit at one end of the rock-hard bed before placing his head down on the pillow at the other.

'The Lebo tried to make conversation, and I kind of just ignored him. I didn't want to talk to anyone. I was trying to take it all in.'

But his new roommate was persistent. 'Do you smoke, bra?'

The question finally drew a response. 'Yeah, man. I'll smoke whatever you got.'

His roommate winked.

The new inmate nodded. *You get it and I'll smoke it.*

'He told me he was getting his meds soon, and he said we would rip into some Buskies [Buscopan].'

He put his head down, a little more at ease now that the ice had been broken. *But what the fuck was a 'Buskie'?*

'Not long after, the doctor came in and gave him his meds. He was given a couple of tablets and pretended to swallow them, but he'd put them under his tongue. He swallowed the water, and after they checked his mouth they shut the door.'

His cellmate spat a couple of white pills, dripping with saliva, onto his palm.

'The pills were called Buscopan, and they were for people with cramps and shit like that. They would give them to inmates who were hanging out from the gear.'

The Buscopan virgin looked at the Lebanese inmate. 'What would I want that shit for?' he said. 'I don't have cramps, bro.'

The Lebanese inmate smiled. 'Trust me, bra,' he said. 'You'll be off ya tree. You got any foils?'

The pair began rummaging around the room, looking for a scrap of aluminum foil. The drugs were useless for a high if you swallowed them in tablet form. But smoked? *Well, you'll soon find out . . .*

They couldn't find any foil. Not a shred.

'We had none, so we had to wait until the dinners came round,' the former inmate continued. 'They came in on a foil tray, you know? To keep the shit food warm.'

The Darcy veteran ripped the tray apart once they slammed down the slop.

'He then took the coating off the tablet, chopped it all up and put it on the foil. He sparked it up and I smoked it.'

The fresh fish exhaled the strange-smelling smoke, which filled the small cell.

And then he collapsed.

'I hit the bed and couldn't move. I was completely paralysed.'

I'm going to die. Fuck! What have I just done?

'My tongue shrivelled up and I had no saliva. The only thing I could move was my eyeballs. I was so fucked up.'

That's when he saw the needle of an old, rusty, bloodied syringe.

'My head was still facing him. I couldn't move, but I could still see okay. I was looking at him and he was having a shot. He had a needle and was injecting up. I'd been around a fair bit of that on the outside, and I've lost a lot of mates to drug overdose, so it makes me very uncomfortable.'

Not just uncomfortable – *fucking flipping out*.

'In my head, I was thinking, *I can't be in a cell with this bloke*. I'd heard about AIDS and the people who will jab you with syringes over nothing. I was fucking flipping out, but I couldn't move. I tried so hard to get up but couldn't. I was pinned to the bed for about an hour.'

Soon he managed to move a toe, a little later a finger, and then his arm.

'Eventually I was able to get up. I was still fucked up, but I managed to get to the basin.'

Vision blurred, limbs barely obeying the signals being sent by his brain, he mashed at a button.

'The shower came on instead of the tap. And the other fella started going off his tits. He was like, "What the fuck? You only get two showers in here a day. You just fucked us." He was tripping out, and I was like, *Oh shit, I've already trod on someone's toes*.'

All the newbie wanted to do was wet his face, hoping that a splash of water would stun him out of his drug-fucked slumber.

'I went back to my bed and laid down again. It was getting dark and I was panicking a bit.'

Yep. The syringe. The dirty, used needle that could turn into a death sentence without notice.

'How could I sleep? There was a syringe in the room, and now he was upset with me. I thought he was going to stab me. So I thought, *Fuck this* . . . and jumped up.'

Crack!

A right to the head.

Bang!

An elbow this time.

Crack!

Another right.

The blows kept on coming, a *shower* of fists.

'I knew I wouldn't be able to sleep with him in the room, so I just gave him a hiding. I flogged him. Then I pulled him off his bed and wrapped him up around the toilet. I left him lying there for about an hour, and then he woke. He got up and came towards me. But I was still awake and saw him coming.'

Crack!

Only one blow this time – a big one, straight to the temple, putting him back to sleep.

But not before the potential syringe-stabbing cellmate screamed.

'He managed to alert the screws. They came in and saw him lying on the floor. They grabbed me and took me out, telling me I was going to another cell. I thought I was going to segro, but they said, "No, we're just putting you in another room."'

Buscopan was recently identified as a major problem in the British prison system. Correctional medical staff sent a letter to authorities in mid-2015, warning them that inmates were crushing up the drug and smoking it.

'It releases scopolamine,' the letter said. 'A known potent hallucinogen.'

A doctor, working in the UK prison system, said he was receiving dozens of requests a day for the drug. A prison anti-drug organisation revealed they were aware of one serious incident where an inmate collapsed after smoking a near-fatal dose of the psychoactive substance.

The over-the-counter drug is still available to inmates in Australian prisons.

Cellmate No.2

Another door slammed and another cellmate sat on a bed – *his* bed.

No. Not again . . .

'There was this fucking hippie-looking guy with long hair and shit in the cell,' the former inmate continued. 'He was in a yoga pose on the bed, making all these weirdo Buddhist-type sounds . . . Umming, ahhing and carrying on.'

What the fuck is this? This place is a freak show.

'Anyway, they shut the door and he started talking to me. He seemed like he was a good bloke. He was pretty normal, talking about shit, and he asked me where I was from. I told him I was from the Central Coast, and he said he was from the Blue Mountains.'

The long-haired hippie nodded. 'So, do you know Rachel?'

What the . . .?

'Nah, man,' our inmate replied. 'I told you I'm from the Central Coast. How the fuck would I know Rachel?'

The yoga man nodded again. 'What about Steve?'

Seriously?

'I told him that I wasn't from the Blue Mountains and that I didn't know Steve. I told him I didn't know anyone he knew.'

But the inmate, no longer doing the full lotus on his cellmate's bed, would not be deterred.

'He kept on asking me if I knew these people. Fucking John, Bill, George . . . He wouldn't shut up. The bloke was a fucking whack job and he started giving me the shits.'

Again, the new inmate started to worry.

'He looked like a tree-hugging, rainforest fuck and was a skinny weed. I could have flogged him, but it doesn't matter how big you are or how good you fight, if you are asleep. I ended up putting it out of my mind because I was fucking tired. I was still fucked up from smoking that shit, and I didn't think he looked like the violent type.'

The hippie stopped rattling off names and asked for a smoke.

'He was out so I gave him one. Then I said, "Shut the fuck up and let me sleep."'

Lights out . . .

He suddenly woke from his slumber, hair tickling his face, a hand rubbing his leg.

'I opened my eyes and he was leaning over me, with his hand on me. I thought he was trying to rape me.'

Crack!

A perfect right hook into the hippie's head.

'That's all it took. He was out.'

45

Turns out the limber, long-haired lout was only after another smoke. He was trying to pull the tobacco pouch from his new cellmate's pocket.

Oh well . . .

'I laid him out next to the cell door and went back to sleep.'

Pppffffftttttt!

Our punchy, desperately tired inmate was woken again – this time by the sound of shit falling on cement. *Slap.*

'I looked up and he was crouching in front of the door doing a shit. He was all crouching-tiger-hidden-dragon laying a log. He was snapping one off at the front door.'

Slap! Slap! Slap!

'I jumped back up and gave the dirty fucker another hiding. For fuck's sake! *What a place!* He then started making all these weird noises and was rolling around in his own shit. He had shit all over him, and I was like, "Get away from me, you cunt. Don't touch me." He had painted himself up and was running around like a lunatic. He then knocked and asked the screws for some toilet paper. I was like, "Bit late now, you cunt." They came, took him out and left me alone.'

Thank fuck.

He finally got back to sleep.

Velcro, Cups and Dribbling Junkies

He woke up again when the cell door cracked opened. The silent night had broken. The morning began with a murmur, a few inmates speaking softly, but soon it erupted into a full-blown roar.

'I remember how it went from being so quiet to so loud,' the new inmate said. 'Everyone got up at the same time and walked out into the wing, and that's when the place just exploded with noise.'

The inmate, sleep-deprived and dopey from the drug he had smoked and the beatings he had delivered, put on his greens and staggered, zombie-like, into the hall.

He was suddenly wide awake.

'I was spinning out when I walked down the stairs. Everyone was wearing Dunlop Volleys with velcro straps instead of laces.' It wasn't the shoes that freaked him out – it was the cups. 'They had these red plastic mugs strapped to the velcro. They'd put the handle on the mug through the strap.'

What the fuck is wrong with these people?

'Seriously, you can only imagine what I was thinking. I was the only one without a cup strapped to his shoe.'

He wondered whether it was some sort of gang thing. Should he go back and get his cup and slap it on his shoe too?

'You get one bowl, one plate and one cup when you arrive. And they're all red plastic. I soon found out that you keep your bowl and your plate in your cell, but you keep your cup on you for drinks throughout the day.'

Water for some, coffee for others and methadone for most.

'I just remember thinking, *What the fuck am I doing here?*'

Then he saw a familiar face.

'I got down to the bottom and I saw some bloke I knew from the streets. This bloke was a real tough cunt – a heavy. But when I saw him there, he was leaning over in a chair, drooling from the mouth. He was fucked. He looked like he'd just had a big shot of heroin and was about to OD. He started falling off the chair. I didn't know what to do. I wanted to help him, but I thought he might not recognise me and snap.'

Against his better judgment, he went to the aid of the once-was-warrior.

'I helped him up and said g'day. He recognised me.'

The former street heavy slumped against the back of his chair, fresh spit dribbling from the corner of his mouth. 'I'm fucked, bro. I've gone downhill, man. This place is killing me. I don't think I'll ever make it out of here.'

The new arrival turned away from the junkie and looked towards the yard.

'There were about 80 blokes in there and it was just tragic. Everyone looked like they were overdosed. All junkies. It was the wing that held everyone who came straight from the street, so they were all hanging out because they weren't getting gear for the first few days. It's the new reception wing, and you're there for four or five days until they work out where to put you.'

An inmate yelled, 'Look at this!' and they all came running.

'Everyone went over to one of the observation cells. They were yelling out to come and have a look. I ran over and there was a transvestite in the cell playing with her tits. She'd had a full boob job and was putting on a show for the lads.

I thought I was in a madhouse. I thought if it was going to be like this for the next decade then I am necking up.'

Yep . . . Get me the fuck out of here.

Race Wars

The former inmate spent five days in hell, surviving syringes and cellmates who shat themselves.

'Go and get your stuff,' a guard said. 'All of it. I'll be standing outside your cell in 15 minutes.'

Finally . . . *But what next?*

'They told me I was going to 9 Wing. That's where all the Asians and Islanders were. I was relieved to be out of the Darcy 1 shithole, but also a bit scared about where I was going next. I didn't know who I was going to run into. I had a lot of previous enemies from the streets.'

Oh well . . . can't be any worse.

'So I psyched myself up and told myself I was ready to deal with anything. I had to, or I was going to die. Someone would kill me or I would kill myself.'

And so began prison life proper . . .

'I got some bad looks when I first arrived because of the way I look. As I mentioned, I look a bit like a Lebo. It was pretty intense when I walked in. They were all staring at me.'

Here we go. I'm about to get bashed. Maybe worse.

'But then someone yelled out my name. A bloke who knew me came up and shook my hand. He told the rest of the yard that I was Islander and I was okay. I was lucky he knew me and yelled out. Otherwise, they would have killed me.'

He knew others in the wing too. And others knew of him.

'One of my coeys [co-offender in a crime] was well known by most in the wing. And they knew I was his boy. That earned me some respect straight up. It was a bit of a green light straightaway. *Thank fuck.*'

He was immediately given the rundown, told the unwritten laws of prison that might just save his life. The criminal code of the convicted certainly wouldn't guarantee his survival, but at least the knowledge would give him a fighting chance.

'The boys gave me the rundown because it wasn't like juvenile jails or the streets,' he continued. 'They told me that if someone was after you, they were coming to kill you – and it was up to you to kill them first. In prison when they say, "I'm going to get you", it means they are going to *kill* you. It's a hit.

'They also told me to keep away from all the other races. They said it's forbidden to even speak to another nasho [nationality]. The only people they said I could talk to aside from fellow Islanders were the Asians, who we shared a wing with, and also the Aussies because they were okay. We ran with them too.'

But the Lebanese? The Aboriginals?

'No way,' he said. 'Not under any circumstance. If that happens, you will be bashed by your own. They also gave me a rundown on the Asians, and they pointed out the head guys and told me not to cross paths with them. Even though we had an arrangement, there was a limit to what you could say to them. You could only go so far with jokes and you couldn't stare at any of them.'

Okay. So don't have anything to do with the Lebanese and Aboriginals. And don't joke about the Asians or stare at them. *That it?*

'There were some other rules from within the Islander group that we also had to follow,' he said. 'There were about 80 in this wing, and they did everything they could to try and keep order. They had to because there was a race war going on and blokes were getting stabbed left, right and centre.

'There were stages and rankings within our own group, and you didn't do a thing without permission. You knew who the main man was, the right-hand man, and so forth. There was a numbering system going down in order. Anytime you had dramas, you would go to the number-five man, who would send it up the chain. They would get back to you with a solution to the problem and tell you what you could or could not do.

'If I went to another wing and punched on without permission, I would be in shit. Say, if I would've gone and hit an Aboriginal, being an Islander, I would have brought unwanted attention to the whole Islander yard. They would have sorted me out by bashing me before sorting out the problem with the other wing. It would depend on how high your ranking was and what sort of person and rep you had as to what your punishment would be. You couldn't go putting the whole Islander yard in a war without getting consent first.

'They told me not to start anything with anyone. You can defend yourself but you can't start something. If you want to start something with someone else – even someone from another wing – then you had to get permission of the corporals, captains and lieutenants.'

Breaching internal yard rules left you at risk of becoming a loner. And that meant you either went into protection or ended up dead.

'They told me not to fuck up in this wing because everyone in here was my back-up. They also said you can never give any cunt up. Ever.'

Race, internal politics and 'dogging' sorted, they then told the new inmate things of lesser importance: what time the food was served, what time lockdown was, what they did to pass the time . . .

My First Shiv

Our convicted murderer waited until all was quiet. Even his cellmate was asleep. The room was dark, with just enough moonlight streaming in through the perspex window for him to see.

He waited and he listened.

All good. No guards. They're probably having a nap in the office.

He pulled the mattress from his bed to expose a sea of metal snakes, all coiled and ready to strike.

'There's a grille under the bed that your mattress lays on,' he said. 'And it's made from metal.'

He had been given instructions earlier that day, a veteran inmate telling him what he needed to do to 'arm up'.

And everyone in here should be 'armed-up'.

'You couldn't break the metal off with your hands – it was too strong. So I grabbed one of my singlets and soaked it in the sink.'

He pressed the right button this time and his cellmate continued dreaming deeply. Then the stealthy prisoner pulled out the piece of broomstick he had snapped off and stashed in his cell.

'I tied the wet singlet around two of the metal bits and tied a knot in it. Then I got the bit of broomstick handle, put it through and started twisting it.'

Snap!

The metal broke under the strain of singlet and stick. His cellmate stirred but did not wake. No footsteps in the hall. No guards rushing towards his door.

'I ended up breaking off three bits of metal, and then I wrapped them up together with some cloth.'

He pulled out the bottle cap he had pocketed at lunch.

'I put it at the base,' he explained. 'To stop [the three pieces of metal] from sliding and to make a bit of a handle. I then used stickers from shampoo bottles, deodorant cans – whatever I had – to stick it all together.'

And that was his shiv, his first makeshift jail weapon. But now he had to hide it. Apparently making the shiv was the easy part.

'I got my hands on the metal bit of a screwdriver. It was just the stick without a handle. I think it was someone else's old shiv, but it was pretty useless as a weapon compared to what we were making by then.'

But it was still a screwdriver.

'I used it to take the light switch cover off and pull out the entire switch. It was still connected by all the wiring, but you could pull it out far enough to expose the cavity in the wall.'

He used some string obtained in the yard to tie his shiv to the wiring. Then he dropped it into the cavity and screwed the cover back on.

Now he was all 'armed-up'. *But why?*

'I just thought I needed one because of the shit I'd seen,' he explained. 'I'd seen an Asian bloke walk out a couple of days before, and he had two knives. He walked up to this bloke and wanted to fight. He handed him one of the shivs and said, 'Let's go.' They fucking stabbed the shit out of each other. There was blood everywhere. That's why I made the knife. I saw how serious it got in there and didn't want to be left without a weapon. I knew I could fight and handle myself, but when you see something like that . . . Well, it's something else. It's beyond fists.'

There were violent men in his wing. Killers . . . *just like him.*

'There were blokes with big reps in there,' he said, 'but not blokes who are famous from the papers. The guy who ran our wing had killed someone outside, and then he killed someone inside. He beat the rap and made it out. But then he killed someone else on the outside and came back in.'

Yep . . . and then he killed inside again.

'This guy has killed about six people, but no one on the outside would have ever heard of him,' he continued. 'He's not known like Milat. There are plenty like that in jail who aren't famous outside but have a high ranking among the crims. These blokes are much tougher and more violent than most of the guys you'd have read about.'

And these were his allies? His back-up? No wonder he made a shiv.

'It was the Lebos and Abos I was really worried about. We were in the middle of a war and I had to arm up to protect myself.'

But how can you stab – or be stabbed – by someone who is locked away in another wing?

'Oh, that's easy. You would cross paths with them all the time. You would see them at visits [the visiting centre where inmates are allowed to sit down with family and friends] mostly, or just come across them on your way somewhere else in the jail. Say you were in 9 or 10 Wing and you had to go to the doctor or something. The screws would come get you and take you there.'

Sometimes there would be one officer escorting the offender, sometimes two.

'You would have to go past 11 Wing and 12 Wing, or 13 Wing and 14 Wing. You were sure to walk past someone on the way. There would be officers with you and officers with the other bloke.' But that didn't matter – as long as you had permission from your 'Wing Boss'. 'You would just run at them and smash them. The screws couldn't stop you.'

Often, at least according to this former inmate, the officers even encouraged it.

'The screws would fuck people up who got smart. Say a Lebo got smart during reception and the screw had the shits with him. The screw could just process him and put him in the Islander yard. He would be bashed, maybe killed. That would shut him up. We knew we had the green light if a Lebo walked into our yard.'

Visiting family and friends was the best time of the week for inmates. It was also the deadliest.

'Most of it happened on the way to or from visits. There were plenty of weapons in visits. There was a bush outside of the visits area, just before you entered. The high-risk guys, the ones dressed in orange, would walk down with escorts. But the greens [normal-classification inmates] would go down there alone. You can walk down by yourself with your knife and put it in the bush while you do your visit. When you go out and the door clicks, you look around and make sure no one is watching. You pick it up and walk back down the corridor, and that's when you pass other guys. That's when you stab them.

'Sometimes you would be told to leave the knife for the high-risk guys. They would get it out of the bush on the way back . . . There were so many stabbings in that corridor.'

No wonder people tried to escape.

4

HELICOPTERS AND HOLLYWOOD
Silverwater

Conning a Conman

He was adamant he could do it.

'Of course I can get you out,' the inmate, who was also a pilot, said. 'It's a piece of piss. Give me 20K and you'll be back with her as soon as I'm released. I'll come back with a helicopter in two months. I'll pick you up and you'll be with her for the rest of your life. Hugging, kissing . . . doing whatever the hell you want.'

John Reginald Killick nodded. 'Maybe.'

Paul Bennett had heard the sad tale – *everyone in the Silverwater Correctional Centre had* – of the past-his-used-by-date thief who went back to his forgotten trade for love; of the 57-year-old inmate who got caught holding up a bank so he could support his Lucy – the tortured, broken woman who came into the visits section of Silverwater and cried uncontrollably.

'I will just die if you don't get out,' she wept. 'He will kill me. I need you . . . I have to get you out . . .'

This the untold story of how an international fugitive (and unlicensed helicopter pilot), famous for duping Russell Crowe into giving him a job before committing a string of serious offences that would see him go on the run for 13 years, would help Killick pull off the world's most daring jail break.

Breaking his 17-year silence, Killick, now 74, finally reveals the full details of how he pulled off a Bonnie-and-Clyde feat for the ages.

Going Straight

Killick had given up on crime.

'There was a new breed,' he said. 'Guys called Chopper, the Runner . . . They had taken over and I was done. I'd spent most of my life in jail and had no intention of going back.'

First jailed in 1966, and then again in 1972, 1981 and 1985, Killick has done some serious time – 30 years in total. He is one of only three men to spend more than four years in Pentridge Prison's dreaded 'H Block'.

Finally free, he had found love with a lady named Lucy Dudko. Seventeen years his junior, she was pretty, passion-ate . . . and *almost* perfect.

'We were having trouble with her ex,' Killick said. 'It was tough on her. But it all went wrong when my [criminal] record was sent all over Australia. Someone saw it in Queensland, where I had done some crimes, and they came up with an old warrant relating back to 1983.'

Killick was suddenly facing more jail time – not a lot, maybe six months at most.

'But for Lucy it was an eternity,' Killick explained. 'I couldn't fight it because it was a warrant for jail. The cops said they were coming back to get me the next day at 9.30am.'

Dudko was desperate. She thought she would die without her man – the aging bank robber still tough as teak.

'She was in a very bad way,' Killick said. 'She was terrified of being without me. She was in the middle of a big custody battle and it was ugly. You have to understand the pressure she was under. She was getting threats and was coming in crying because she was so afraid. She was getting phone calls at 3am and being called a bitch in Russian. They would say, "We are going to get you, bitch." She thought she was dead.'

Killick had met Lucy Jane Dudko at a party in Sydney in 1995.

'Lucy was intelligent,' he said fondly. 'And she was artistic . . . and boy, was she sexy.'

Killick was finally free after a Queensland court had given him immediate parole, despite being slapped with a 32-month sentence after pleading guilty to the armed robbery in 1983. He'd fled Queensland following the reprieve and moved to Canberra; away from criminal associates and cities filled with temptation; away from Sydney, Melbourne and Brisbane and the guys who could get him guns and gigs with the promise of ill-gotten gains.

But he went back to Sydney for 'just some party', and there she was . . . the slender, blonde, spectacle-wearing librarian. Originally from Russia, Lucy had moved to Sydney from Moscow in 1993.

She's perfect. And she will be mine.

'We just hit it off and ended up exchanging numbers,' he recalled of the night. 'She didn't ring, but I ended up calling her a couple of times. That's how it started, and it went on from there.'

Turns out there was a little problem, though: Lucy was married.

The daughter of a former soviet air force helicopter commander – *yep, a helicopter pilot* – Lucy had immigrated with her Russian husband, Alexei Dudko, a respected and well-paid scientist.

The couple had a daughter named Marsha, and on the surface all was well. Lucy was studying for a doctorate in history at Macquarie University. Bright and bubbly, most thought she had found the perfect life in the land of opportunity after fleeing Russia.

She hadn't.

'She was terribly unhappy and that marriage was dead,' Killick said. 'She wanted to split from him. So that wasn't a problem, as far as me beginning a relationship with her. She told me she had wanted to leave him for a long time. They actually came to Australia because they were leaving her father in Russia, and he hated [Alexei]. He was a tough old bugger and he would have ended it, so that's why [Alexei] packed everything up and moved her to Australia.'

She left Alexei and started seeing John, his constant calls finally paying off. They soon moved in together.

And that's when things got ugly.

'We were going pretty well,' Killick said. 'And then we started having a bit of trouble with Alexei.'

A child made the situation explosive, and an ugly custody battle ensued over their daughter.

'He couldn't handle not being with [Lucy],' Killick said. 'We had the girl [Marsha] for five days a week, and he had her for two. It was really tough on her.'

Alexei claimed, in an interview with the *Sydney Morning Herald* in 2006, that he never wanted to challenge for custody and start a war.

'I didn't intend to be a single parent,' Alexei told reporter Eamonn Duff from his home in Russia, where he returned in 2003. 'When we separated, I thought Marsha would live with her mother. Only the prospect of having her live with Mr Killick made me struggle for custody.'

Things got nasty.

And it was a widely distributed document that started the stunning series of crimes, crying and cells that would lead to Australia's – if not the world's – greatest escape.

'Killick's criminal record surfaced in the area where he lived, including the school Marsha attended. It also came to the attention of all the police stations and courts around Australia.

'They saw it up in Queensland and came up with the old warrant from the offence in 1983,' Killick said.

Knock! KNOCK!

Killick opened the door.

'John,' said the Australian Federal Police constable, who knew Killick well. 'I'm sorry to do this to you, mate. But . . .' He produced a neatly pressed A4 piece of paper, unfolded it and presented it to the shocked man standing at the door.

'This is a warrant from Queensland for your arrest. Apparently you breached conditions of your parole for that robbery in 1983. And . . . well . . . sorry, mate – you're going back to jail.'

Killick turned white. '1983?' he said. *'Seriously?* You're kidding me, right?'

Afraid not, John. You're going back to jail.

'He was very apologetic,' Killick continued. 'He said they thought it was ridiculous too, but they couldn't do anything about it. He said they had to act on it.'

Killick looked back at the cop. 'Is there anything I can do? Can't I challenge it?'

The burly man in blue shook his head slowly. 'It's not a court warrant, mate,' he said. 'It's a jail warrant. You owe them time and that's the end of the matter.'

Killick closed the door, shaking, sad, sorry and completely stunned.

The Queensland Parole Board alleged that Killick, who

was allowed to serve his parole in New South Wales, breached his conditions in 1993 by committing a firearms offence in that state and failing to report it.

'I was told they would be coming back to pick me up at 9.30 the next morning,' Killick said.

'I called my lawyer and he confirmed that it wasn't something I could fight because I owed them that time.'

Yep . . . they were coming back. And after breakfast he would be put in cuffs and carted back to Queensland to resume his all-too-familiar life in a cell.

Bang, Bang, Bang . . . Back in Business.
Killick recalled the conversation he'd had with Lucy. The one that started with, 'Why were the cops just here?'

'I told Lucy, and she told me I couldn't go to jail,' Killick said. 'She was terrified of being without me because of the other guy. She would have been fucked without me, so we decided there and then to pack up and leave. From that moment on we were fugitives. We had no money and I felt I had no options but to go back to what I did best.'

Yep . . . back to hitting banks.

Killick resumed his career in crime, the one he had started on when he was a teenager selling raffle tickets with the promise of a non-existent prize.

'I felt concerned about the possibility of leaving my partner,' Killick said in an affidavit letter tendered in court. 'And I felt no matter what I did I would end up back in jail. As such, I went on the run.'

'I got away with the first [bank robbery],' he said. 'That all went fine, but then I hit another one in January and got caught.'

Almost old enough to get a pensioner's discount in a McDonald's drive-thru, Killick was crippled by rust and a reticence to rob. He was arrested in Bowral on 20 January 1999, after stealing $23,000 from the National Australia Bank.

'I was past it,' he admitted. 'There was a dye bomb in the cash I stole during the second robbery, and an off-duty copper to boot.'

'Stuff off, you idiot!' Killick screamed at the cop who bravely gave chase. 'This is a real gun and I *will* kill you.'

Only a car separated the copper from the on-the-run con.

'That's when he decided to pick up a big rock and throw it at me,' Killick recalled.

Mmm . . . taking a rock to a gunfight?

Bang!

Killick let off a round.

'I shot it into the ground. It was a warning shot. Something to show him the gun was real and that I was willing to use it.'

But the cop refused to let the robber go.

'I ended up having to fire three shots – one into the ground and two over his head. They were at different times, and I was always aiming to miss . . . They charged me with shooting with intent to kill, but that was bullshit and we eventually fought it and won. There were other witnesses who saw exactly what had happened and they backed my version of events.'

Killick was far from happy after learning of the shoot-to-kill charge. He bumped into the officer at the police station shortly after his arrest.

'I said, "Mate, if I was trying to shoot you, you would be dead."'

The money from the robbery was never recovered.

'How about that?' Killick said. 'I can't work out for the life of me how 23K just vanished into thin air.'

Killick was also charged with another armed bank robbery at Picton – the one he 'got away with' – and for firearms offences in Queanbeyan.

Soon Killick was back behind bars. He was incarcerated in the MRRC at Silverwater, awaiting three trials in three courts, the most serious at Wollongong District Court, where he would face up to two charges of armed robbery and one of shooting with intent to kill.

And that's when Lucy began to beg and ball . . . a broken woman, now fearing for her life.

Desperate, Desolate but Doomed?

There is no suggestion that the intimidating calls Lucy received at 3am came from her estranged husband, Alexei, but Lucy's father – the elite helicopter squadron commander – confirmed his daughter was living in fear.

Vitaly Zhdanov told the *Australian* that his daughter had been 'living on the edge of desperation for years'.

'We were ready for something,' Zhdanov said. 'But not this.'

Lucy had expressed fears for her safety in a series of letters to him, claiming the Australian Russian community made her life difficult following the separation and when she began a relationship with Killick in 1996.

Lucy was described by a social worker as a 'desperate woman with only one person left in her life' after Alexei took full custody of daughter, Marsha.

Lucy Dudko is understood to have visited Killick at least 20 times during his incarceration at the MRRC, and she would write him a letter every night.

'She wanted me out,' Killick said. 'She was alone and needed me. We talked about it during every visit and spoke about how it could be done.'

Killick's history of escape and attempted escape seemed an impossible hurdle. *Seemed . . .*

'I had little hope,' Killick said. 'I was classified "extreme risk" because I'd escaped a couple of other jails and also had a couple of failed attempts.'

Killick recalled his 1984 jailbreak in Queensland. 'I used a toy gun to break out of the hospital.' He had faked an illness – and eye injury – so he could be moved to the less-secure prison hospital in Brisbane.

Reports claimed his girlfriend at the time had used

a 9mm Luger pistol to threaten guards and secure Killick's release while he was being escorted to the medical facility.

Wrong.

'Nothing like that happened at all,' Killick claimed. 'For starters, I escaped from the hospital and not from an escort. And secondly, the gun wasn't real – it was a replica. [My girl-friend] had nothing to do with it except for giving it to me.'

Killick claimed she'd purchased a 'replica Derringer' from a store in Fortitude Valley, Brisbane.

'I got her to drill a hole in the middle because it was blocked,' Killick continued. 'I wouldn't lie to you about any of this because I have nothing to gain from not telling the truth. It was a replica pistol. She drilled a hole in the middle of it and painted it black.'

It certainly looked real because the guard, the one with the fully loaded, *functional* pistol dropped his gun and allowed Killick to run.

'She slipped [the replica gun] to me during a visit to the hospital,' Killick said. 'She gave it to me in a newspaper. I was in handcuffs at the time, but I managed to pull the gun from the paper.'

Killick then pointed the completely useless piece of metal at the unsuspecting officer.

'He went for his gun and I said, "Do it and you're dead." He dropped it, so I spun around and ran off. They never even came after me.'

Killick also escaped from a jail in Perth and almost killed a guard in the infamous Pentridge Prison in his failed attempt in Victoria . . . *but more on that later.*

So how the hell was he going to escape the maximum-security prison at Silverwater, which was almost as secure as Goulburn's escape-proof Supermax?

'I was to be escorted by armed guards to court visits because of my classification, so I couldn't do a runner,' Killick said. 'I told Lucy they were all over me and on to me. I thought the hospital was the only chance. We had all these conversations in visits, but it seemed impossible. Even escaping from the hospital was a one-in-a-million chance, and there was no way of digging out of there or jumping a fence.'

Enter the man who conned a movie star . . .

Plotting, Planning and Pilots

'You know that bloke who conned Russell Crowe?' Killick asked. 'That Bennett? Well, we got talking one day and he told me he was a helicopter pilot.'

Before Paul Bennett – also known as Paul James, David Kite, Dennis Kite, Paul Lochead and David Hanson – landed on Crowe's Coffs Harbour property in a helicopter and asked for a job, before he was hired because the movie man thought he was 'cheeky', and then was sacked for selling secrets about Meg Ryan, the hell-raising pilot was locked up with Killick.

'There were 20 wings in Silverwater,' Killick said, 'and this guy ends up in my wing . . . A one-in-20 chance. And he says he can get me out.'

Yep. 20K. Ten thousand up front and you're back with Lucy.

'He told me he could get me out by helicopter,' Killick continued. 'He wanted cash up front. I knew he was a conman and that he would rip me off.'

But then a light bulb went off.

'I thought if we gave him a bit he might tell us how it could be done. So Lucy put some money in his pocket and I got to pick his brains.'

Heights? *Check*. Speeds? *Check*. Times? *Check*.

'The most important thing he told me was about the [emergency] transponder. If we hadn't known about that then we wouldn't have made it.'

Killick grilled Bennett for a month.

He was conning a conman . . .

'I told Lucy it could be done,' Killick said. 'And we decided it *would* be done.'

Every detail was intricately plotted . . . It had to be perfect. No one in Australia had ever pulled off a helicopter escape. And this was no prison farm. This was Silverwater – the place where serial killers, child murderers and drug lords were locked up while they awaited trial, most likely to be sentenced.

'I got her to do a test run. She said it was great and told me it would work. The only thing was that I had to make sure I was on the oval. There were so many lockdowns, but I had to be sure I was on the oval when she got there. There was always a risk that I could be locked in my cell and it would all be for nothing. How would that have been for standing up a date? She hijacks a helicopter for me and I'm not there? I wouldn't have been very popular.'

D-Day

THWAAT!

Metal on metal, the bullet won . . . smashing through the helicopter's landing skid.

'I heard the bullet,' Killick recalled of his escape.

Thwaat! Thwaat! Two more.

The guards opened fire as the hijacked helicopter hovered over the yard.

'Lucy and the hijacked pilot, Tim Joyce, came into the yard but never landed,' Killick said. 'The chopper just hovered a metre or so off the ground. I had been waiting, and there would've been about a dozen choppers that came over that morning because of the Olympic Games. I didn't think they would have attracted that much attention because there were always a lot of choppers around.

'The Kooris (Indigenous inmates) were playing footy when they came. I don't think they even stopped.'

Joyce tried to tip the prison guards off. Little did he know it could have cost him his life.

'He didn't come straight in like he should've,' Killick said. 'He circled for too long and alerted them, which gave them time to run off and get their guns. Anyway, they ended up shooting at us. I got inside and I heard *thwaat, thwaat, thwaat.*'

Three shots – high-calibre bullets shot from big guns – were fired. One smacked dirt, another the landing skid, and the last missed a steering cable by centimetres – a hit that could have sent the helicopter crashing into the ground, killing them all.

'As far as I know, the pilot ended up suing and getting some money. He would have never been shot at if he did what he was told. I thought about suing them for shooting too.'

Lucy and the pilot made two failed attempts to land before finally busting him out and flying over near Macquarie Park.

'She had a car there, but she had forgotten the keys. So we had to hijack a car at gunpoint . . . I ended up getting another two years for that when I eventually got caught.'

Tim Joyce, 43 at the time of the escape, was working as a pilot for Helicopters Pty Ltd, a company specialising in taking tourists on joy flights. And in 1999, with the Sydney Olympics just a year away, business was booming.

'Take me to the stadium,' the Germans, Chinese, English and soon a *Russian* would say. 'I want to see Olympic Park.'

Joyce's main craft was a three-seat Bell helicopter, based at Bankstown Airport.

'We were doing a joy flight over the city,' Joyce recalled of the woman who claimed to be German but spoke with a heavy Russian accent. 'And she wanted to fly over the stadium.'

Yes, the stadium that was conveniently just a stone's throw away from the MRRC.

'She seemed to be looking ahead as we were tracking towards the stadium,' Joyce continued. 'I thought she was looking at the Olympic Village.'

But Lucy wasn't interested in observing the sprawling complex of apartments where those vying for gold would live . . . She had her eye on the prison.

'That's the Olympic Village construction site,' Joyce remembered saying. 'But then she looked towards Silverwater and asked if it was the prison.'

Can we have a look at that?

'It was a fairly normal request because people are interested in prisons,' Joyce continued. 'So we flew around it.'

Lucy then asked Joyce to descend. *To fly lower. To fly her to her lover.*

'Nah,' he'd said. 'We can't do that. It's restricted airsp–' He stopped mid-sentence, a pistol now pressed against his head.

This is a hijack. You will land it in that yard. The one right there. Do it now!

'I thought it might have been a toy gun,' Joyce said. 'She pulled it out of her purse while I was looking away.'

Joyce was stunned, but his survival instinct kicked in and his brain automatically told his body what it had been trained to do.

'I went to hit the hijack alert on the transponder,' Joyce continued. 'But she was right onto that. She waved the pistol at me to stop, so I did. Then she ripped my headset off so I had no way of communicating.'

Joyce looked at the slight lady.

'I initially thought about overpowering her,' Joyce said. 'But this woman was also shaking and scared and – who knows – maybe even schizo.' And then there was the gun pointed towards his face. 'I realised that this was all very well-planned and that she was indeed serious. I tried to calm her down. I turned around, smiled at her and said, "Look, don't worry, she'll be right."'

And the helicopter commenced its descent.

Corrective Services alleged that Lucy had handed Killick a gun before – *thwaat, thwaat, thwaat* – the three shots were fired at the helicopter.

Some reports claim the aircraft landed and several prisoners tried to join the threesome in their own spur-of-the-moment bid for freedom.

'Crap,' Killick said. 'As I mentioned, the guys in the yard barely stopped playing footy.'

Luger still staring him in the face – and now a maximum-security prisoner capable of who-knows-what in the cabin – Joyce took off, no doubt shitting himself as rifles rattled and bullets threatened to blow his helicopter to bits.

46 Days with Lucy

'You *what*?' Killick said, the jubilation of seeing the lover who had just set him free suddenly gone. 'You lost the *keys*?'

Meticulously planned and so far so good, aside from the pot shots and not entirely cooperative pilot, things suddenly turned to shit. Lucy couldn't find the keys to the getaway car – a 1986 Mitsubishi Sigma station wagon – that she had stashed in the bush.

Police would have no idea what to think when they found the car in bushland near Terry Hills on 2 March.

'This is our strongest lead,' said a detective at the time. 'This car is going to tell us something about their movements, if not about them.'

The car wasn't going to tell them shit.

'She'd bought the car about a month before,' said Killick. 'It was all part of the plan.'

Without the getaway car, they started to panic. *What do we do now? Are we done?*

'We decided we had to jack a car. It wasn't what we planned, but we had little choice.'

Killick was forced to think quickly. He looked down, surveyed the scene rushing past, and found a strip of green right near a busy road.

'Down there,' he said, waving his gun. 'Land it right there.'

Joyce did what he was told and brought the helicopter to the ground with precision, landing on Christie Park oval, North Ryde.

'Get out,' Lucy demanded. 'You're coming with us.'

But Killick shook his head. 'We don't need a hostage. He's done his job.'

Killick ordered Joyce to kill the engine before tying him up, using cord found in the helicopter. His legs were bound so he couldn't run.

But Lucy and John *could* run, though driving would be easier and they needed a car right then.

Peter Bax was motoring down the road when he saw the slender, well-dressed blonde waving him down, looking a little distressed. Killick wasn't far behind.

'I assumed they wanted to ask for directions,' Bax said during a subsequent trial. 'So I wound down the window.'

Killick pushed past Lucy and stuck his head into the car. 'We have a bit of a problem,' he said politely . . . at least at first. 'Can you take us somewhere?'

Bax paused in thought. He was about to respond when the softly spoken man stuck a gun in his face.

'If you don't, then I will shoot.' Killick, no longer the gentleman, demanded.

Bax – the good Samaritan who'd stopped to help a stranded stranger – was stunned. He was frozen with fear as Killick opened the passenger door and climbed into the front seat while his lover jumped into the back.

'North Sydney,' Killick urged. 'Drive.'

Lucy and Killick said little during the 40-minute drive.

'The man asked her if she had any money,' Bax recalled. 'She whispered something around seven dollars.'

Killick asked Bax a question before issuing a threat. 'Do you have kids? Well, keep calm, do what I tell you and you'll be okay. If not, I will shoot you in the knee.'

Bax was terrified but he managed to stay calm.

'Out,' Killick ordered once they'd arrived and parked in the shadows of the Sydney Harbour Bridge.

The bank robber then jumped into the driver's seat and took off.

'Just one night, please,' said Lucy Dudko before paying $62 in cash. It was 2pm on Friday, 7 May 1999.

ID?

'No, sorry. Don't have any,' she said while looking down at the check-in form. 'I lost my purse and haven't got my cards back yet.'

Lucy, pen in hand, began scribbling on the sheet: *Name of Occupants?* Mr and Mrs M.G. Brown. *Address?* 1/11 Second Avenue, Merrylands.

The manager of Bass Hill Tourist Park in south-west Sydney, Phillip Taylor, suspected the woman was being sneaky.

Probably just another married woman having an affair . . .

Lucy was no longer blonde, her hair now bob-length and black.

Taylor handed her a key. 'Cabin 14. Enjoy your stay.'

Killick was not seen until dusk. Taylor saw a man arguing with a taxi driver before entering her cabin.

Yep. Certainly an affair.

And it was. But Mr and Mrs M.G. Brown weren't sneaking from spouses, they were hiding from the cops, now 45 days on the run.

They would make it to 46 . . . just.

'Surrender!' the heavily armed officer screamed, the loud-speaker turning his already booming voice into a fearsome roar. 'Come out slowly, with your hands in the air.'

Stunned tourists and residents at Bass Hill Tourist Park, rudely awoken in the middle of the night, began peeking out windows and barely cracked doors.

What they saw was simply frightening; bulletproof vests

and polycarbonate riot shields, floodlights and the roaming red dots of laser-sighted rifles.

The general continued to shout: 'Mr John Killick and Mrs Lucy Dudko, we have a warrant for your arrest. Come out now.'

The boss was flanked by an army from the State Protection Group (SPG). The most lethal and highly trained members of the New South Wales police force were armed with tactical shotguns, M16 semi-automatic rifles and UMP submachine guns equipped with flashlights, laser sights and a full magazine of .45-calibre bullets that could be fired at the rate of 700 rounds per minute.

The weapons were drawn and aimed at Cabin 14. There would be no miraculous escape this time. Killick and Dudko had just two options: *surrender or die.*

With more than a dozen SPG officers about to bang down his door, Killick surrendered, walking out of the cabin at 2.30am wearing blue shorts, a red shirt and thongs.

'Hands up!' the boss screamed and Killick complied. 'Walk slowly forward until I tell you to stop.'

Killick was ordered to lie face-down on the asphalt near the entrance to the park. Then the SPG pounced. He was soon cuffed, shackled and in the back of an armoured van.

Lucy Dudko – aka Mrs Brown – walked out five minutes later, arms raised, wearing jeans and a t-shirt. She was cuffed and collared without incident. After 46 days on the run, they were done. Busted. Police entered the cabin and confiscated everything they owned . . . two overnight bags half-filled with clothes. *Oh, and a Luger semi-automatic pistol and a double-barrelled replica Derringer.*

The police located the most wanted couple in Australia after a man, abducted at gunpoint in Melbourne, had driven our very own Bonnie and Clyde to Sydney in his Ford Falcon. Set free after his 880-kilometre drive with a gun jammed in the side of his head, he raced to the closest police station and told them his tale, which ended with Killick opening the door and dumping him on the street – but not before he was forced to take them to a Hungry Jack's for a feed.

Or so the man claimed . . .

'He was never our prisoner,' Killick said. 'For crying out loud, he came into Hungry Jack's with us for a meal. How could he be our hostage when all three of us were sitting around kids eating a meal?'

Killick said the man had agreed to drive them from Sydney to Melbourne for a fee.

'The bloke was a complete liar and fabricated the whole story because we didn't pay him,' Killick said. 'He was never a hostage and we didn't kidnap him. That's why [the kidnapping charge] was thrown out of court. *Jeez* . . . I would have got 57 years if the judge convicted me of that too.'

Killick maintained that the man, spurned by Killick's failure to come up with the promised cash, sold information to the media to make up for the money he had been denied.

'He was a liar and ended up disgraced,' Killick said. 'We were supposed to pay him, and Lucy went out to get the money from a bloke. She went to meet him at Terrey Hills, but he wasn't there. When she came back, I had to go and tell him I couldn't pay him.'

That's when the driver started making threats.

'He knew who we were, of course,' Killick said. 'And he threatened to go to the media and give us up for a big pay cheque. He was just going to say he had spotted us near the Hungry Jack's, but he ended up claiming that we had kidnapped him. I guess he thought he would get more money that way. He gave an exact description of us and told them we'd let him go after eating.

'He didn't go directly to the cops. He went to Channel Nine so he could make cash. He didn't know where we were staying, but it wasn't hard for the police to figure out once they were given our current descriptions and last known whereabouts.'

In the end it was a Whopper with cheese, fries, Coke and a spurned, cashless driver that finally got Bonnie and Clyde caught.

Regrets and Apologies.

Now 74 and a free man – but not free from regret – Killick admitted he used Lucy Dudko to break him out of prison.

'I shouldn't have led her into it, and it was my great regret that she went to jail,' Killick said. 'I did use her to get me out, and I do regret it, but what people don't understand is that Lucy and I were together for three years. She was my partner. We worked as a team, and everything I did was well discussed. We talked this [escape] out, and she was as keen on it as I was. She knew what the risks were and she didn't care. It would have been better if I hadn't of done it and she wouldn't have gone to jail, but who knows what would have happened to her. I would have done a lot less time, that's for sure. I paid for it, and I'm still paying for it – I still can't get out of the state.

'But we were partners in crime.'

Killick was sentenced to 28 years for his string of offences, which included armed robbery, escape and shooting with intent to kill. Judge Barry Mahoney said he had little chance of 'rehabilitation' and imposed the hefty sentence during the highly publicised trial.

'He loved me,' Killick said sarcastically. 'He actually gave me 39 years, which was the highest ever sentence handed out by the district court. But then he reduced it to 28 by saying, "Mr Killick has won himself currency by co-operating with his evidence regarding the Mittagong bank robbery." So I only got 28 . . . I'm a lucky guy!'

Killick may have been sentenced to 28 years, but impeccable behavior, compliance with programs and the help he gave other inmates saw him earn parole on 15 April 2014.

Well, sort of . . .

'I was released from the Dawn de Loas minimum-security prison straight after being parolled,' Killick said. 'But I was arrested at the gate and taken straight back to Silverwater.'

Mmmm. Back to the MRRC, the jail he famously escaped.

'Thankfully, I got bail after just one night. I was taken there for an extradition order that Queensland had put on me. A magistrate took a punt on me, and he was the one who organised the bail.'

Killick thought he was free. But he wasn't.

'I fought that extradition order for three months,' Killick said of the old parole breach relating all the way back to 1984, the one that forced him to flee with his lover, Lucy. The one that inspired the great escape. 'But eventually I lost and was sent back to Queensland, where I served six months in the Woodford Correctional Centre.'

Killick wasn't happy about serving the extra time.

'I think they made it tough for an old guy,' he said after finally being released – for good – in January 2015. 'But I'm not complaining. They obviously had their reasons. As far as I'm concerned, we'll call it quits.'

Losing Lucy

John Killick and Lucy Dudko are now estranged.

'She doesn't want anything to do with me,' he said. 'She's moved on. I've spoken to her but she said it's too painful. I respect that. For me . . . well, I know I did lots of wrong things. I just want to use whatever time I have left to make up for that.

'Legally, I can see her, but I need her permission. I spoke to her last year before I went back to prison and she was pretty receptive. But then she had a change of heart and I think some people got in her ear. When I got out, her number had changed. She said she would only get in trouble seeing me and that she needed to leave it behind.

'She wants to leave it all in the past; the memories are too painful. I was hoping we would be friends. I don't know about a love reunion, but I certainly wanted to have some sort of relationship with her. I know she's very strong in the church and that she has been back to Russia. I know she is still very stressed.'

Lucy – or 'Red Lucy', as she was dubbed by the press – was released from prison on 8 May 2006. She served seven years of her ten-year sentence for her role in both the escape and the subsequent crimes while on the run.

Dudko was described as a model inmate who performed 'maintenance and garden work' at the Dillwynia Correctional Centre in Western Sydney, and she also completed a desktop publishing course.

Lucy turned to God . . . and away from John. She has since changed her name and is now living on the far north coast of New South Wales in a tightly knit church-going community.

As for the brazen Bennett, the Kiwi fantasist who told a British court he had been kidnapped while working for the CIA in South Africa and was charged with at least three counts of fraud while working as a pilot for Russell Crowe? He was finally captured in February 2015, sailing a stolen yacht in Broken Bay, near Palm Beach, with his partner in crime, Simone Wright.

Bennett had fled Australia and committed a series of offences in New Zealand before piloting the yacht back to Sydney.

He was locked up in the John Morony Correctional Complex near Windsor, where he was awaiting trial when this chapter was written.

And the hijacked helicopter? Believe it or not, he and Killick are now friends.

'I spoke to him last year,' Killick said of Tim Joyce. 'We actually had a beer together and he wanted to drive me home, but he couldn't because I had an electronic monitor on and was restricted in where I could and couldn't go. I have his number and talk to him from time to time. He's living in Fiji now and has set up a successful helicopter business over there.'

And guess what? There isn't a jail in sight . . .

5

THE ALLEGED HITMAN AND UNDISPUTED HARDMAN

Goulburn, Nowra and the MRRC

Meet Goldie

The caged gorilla is standing still, looking out the gate towards the row of heavily fortified metal doors on the opposite side of the concrete landing. Bald head down, he takes two steps back before taking two forward, returning to his original position at the mouth of the 3 metre by 2 metre 'holding cell', all wire, concrete and nothing-to-do.

There are three other men in this zoo-like pen – though it's not fit for even a gorilla. They are dressed in green pants and jumpers, except for the giant, who is now nodding to himself, and stands out with his shorts and shin-high white socks.

One of the inmates sticks to himself, staring down at nothing. The other stands in the corner where the wire mesh meets concrete. He appears to be talking to the third prisoner – the one with his back firmly planted against the wall.

The monstrous man turns, slowly and silently. He stares at Mr Back-against-the-wall. But only for a second.

Crack!

The bald behemoth strikes, unleashing a right hook into the man's jaw. The punch is a contradiction: so quick, so nimble, yet so heavy and full of force. The power in the punch sends the unsuspecting inmate first into the wall and then to the floor.

But he should have known it was coming . . .

He lands on his bum.

Thud! A short right to the head.

Whack! Another lightning right, full of force.

Crack! A left this time, the attacker changing tack as his victim raises his left arm in what proves to be a hopeless attempt to protect his face.

The attacker – as fast as he is big – opens up and unleashes all his might. First a heaving right hook, followed by another, and then another. The last punch is as powerful as the first. Every strike connects with face, knuckles cracking chin, nose and eye.

He finishes the flurry with a left and two rights.

But this isn't over. Not yet.

Stomp! He lifts his sneaker high into the air and smashes more face with his foot.

Stomp! He smiles while crushing his shoe into skull.

'Over here,' yells the second inmate, who has urinated in his pants, green dacks now dark with stinking piss. He waves frantically, thinking he could be next. *'Quick!'*

The attack suddenly stops. The caged gorilla turns his back on his prey, who is now bashed beyond recognition. Again he stands still and stares, this time not at fortified metal doors but at the three guards rushing towards the cell.

The officer, the one with the keys, unlocks the cage.

Here we go. Hope we don't have to fight him. Three-on-one? Back-up better be on its way.

The giant ignores the trio of officers, and in return they ignore him as he slowly walks out of the cell. He takes one last look at his victim before walking down the landing and voluntarily putting himself in a vacant cell.

Thank fuck. No fight.

Meet Rodney 'Goldie' Atkinson . . . an alleged hitman for hire and an undisputed enforcer, feared by both prisoners and guards alike. In his first-ever interview, the Nomad bikie gang original and Brothers 4 Life heavy broke his silence to reveal the shocking truth about prison and speak about segregation, gangs and the day he beat, belted and stomped a cowardly killer called Tony Halloun.

'At first they tried to say that I bashed him because he was Christian and I was Muslim,' Atkinson said. 'But that had nothing to do with it. I just bashed him because he was a sick fuck who deserved to get flogged. He was bragging about the crime he'd committed. He was bragging about what he was in for. I overheard what he was saying and I just couldn't let it go.'

Slapping a Sicko

Tony Halloun, a struggling concreter, screamed at the doctor.

'Get the cash now!' he demanded, confronting his family physician in the doctor's quaint Croydon surgery. 'I know you have it. You're rich. You owe me $3,500 and I need it NOW.'

Dr Khalil Qidwai stood firm. 'You've already been paid for the work you've done. You will be given the rest of the money when you are finished.'

Halloun stared down his doctor. 'I'll win in the end.'

Halloun had been employed by Dr Qidwai, who had treated the concreter's family for 30 years, to renovate a driveway at the doctor's Henley home – a mansion in Sydney's affluent lower North Shore known as 'Burnham Castle'.

Weeks had passed since the Pakistani-born doctor had employed the Lebanese Christian to fix his driveway and do other work, but the job was not done.

In fact, he had barely begun.

And now he was in the respected GP's surgery demanding thousands in cash.

Halloun would later claim that he had calmly asked for the money to buy besser blocks he needed for the job. He said the doctor offered to pay by credit card or cheque, which made him feel both 'disappointed and angry', because he made more money from cash jobs.

Halloun was desperate. A man with no history of violence, the concreter was sinking in a sea of debt. The 36-year-old father of three had just placed his business in liquidation and was at least $96,000 in the red.

15 June 2012. The day after Halloun confronted him and declared, 'I will win,' Dr Qidwai, a devout Muslim, arrived home to find it swarming with police and lit up by frightening blue and red flashes.

What's all this? What's happened?

He was soon told that his 65-year-old wife, Shahnaz, who had taken the day off from assisting her husband at the Croydon surgery, was dead. The doctor's daughter Maha, 28, had found her body at about 2pm. The university student would be left scarred for life after seeing her dead mother bloodied and beaten on the bedroom floor.

'This is a homicide,' said a paramedic to his colleague after seeing a red footprint next to the bludgeoned body. 'She's been murdered. This is a crime scene.'

The ambulance officer tiptoed out of the room, careful not to contaminate evidence as he left the body behind.

Tears flowed down the faces of family and neighbours as police officers lashed the home with yellow tape. Dr Qidwai and his son had to be restrained as they pushed and pleaded to see Shahnaz's body. *To find out what had happened to their wife and mum.*

They would later learn that the mother of four, grandmother of seven, had died after suffering a series of blunt-force injuries to her head. Shahnaz had also sustained significant trauma to her chest and ribs in an apparent robbery gone wrong.

She had been killed for a necklace and $3,420.

4 December 2012. Tony Halloun was sentenced for the murder of Shahnaz Qidwai. Convicted of the shocking crime three months earlier, Justice Lucy McCallum imposed a maximum sentence of 24 years for the murder that had shocked the nation, especially the Islamic community, many of whom had been lifelong patients of the doctor and his loving wife.

'He attacked a vulnerable woman in her own home in a panic when Mrs Qidwai found him stealing cash,' the judge had said. 'I am satisfied the offender formed an intention to steal from the house, but I doubt he intended to kill Mrs Qidwai.'

And that's why the enforcer known as Goldie bashed Halloun in Goulburn Jail, when Australia's newest 'granny killer' was 'accidentally' put in the wrong yard.

Halloun had arrived at Goulburn Jail, the most feared prison in Australia, a marked man. He was terrified of being bashed, belted – maybe even killed – because of the outrage caused by his crime.

'Protection, please,' he asked as soon as he entered the jail. 'I believe I have many enemies here.'

The guard did not disagree – how could he, after Justice McCallum had said, 'In the particular circumstances of this case, I am persuaded that the offender's time in prison will be more onerous than many prisoners in the general prison population.' So it was off to the boneyard for this killer, his crime so abhorrent that other killers would, well . . . kill him on sight.

'Some were even talking about cutting his head off,' Goldie Atkinson recalled, 'saying ridiculous stuff, like they would cut through his neck with sharpened plastic and razor blades.'

Goldie, regarded as one of the toughest men in the prison at the time, didn't know if it was a coincidence or a set-up.

'I had just come out of a visit and was waiting in a cage where you are put after your visit,' Atkinson said. 'You wait there until a screw comes and gets you and takes you back to your wing. I walked into the cage and there were a couple of blokes there . . . One of them was Halloun, the scumbag who'd killed the old woman. Word had been put out that he was to be got.'

Halloun, who'd had his request for protection approved, should not have not been put in a cage with a prisoner from gen pop [general population]. Especially with a thrashing machine like Goldie.

'He had just been in a visit too,' Atkinson said. 'But for some reason he was in a cage with me. They either made a mistake by putting him in there, or they put him in on purpose because they wanted me to get him.

'Personally, I think it was a set-up. I was classified as Extreme High Risk, so I shouldn't have even been with anyone from the get-go, let alone a protection Dog.'

Atkinson had said nothing at first, a million thoughts – all of them violent – running through his head: *Are they trying to get me to bash him so they can charge me? Do they want me to bash him? What will the other inmates think if I don't bash him?*

All those voices in his mind were silenced when Halloun started telling a fellow inmate in the cage how he had killed the elderly woman.

'I heard him bragging and I couldn't let it go,' Atkinson said. 'I just couldn't help thinking that it could have been my partner and my daughter. To hear how a daughter found her mother lying bashed dead on the floor. Well, in my books, you don't go near women and children.

'He had to pay.'

That is why Halloun unleashed. Not, as he would later claim, because he was a Lebanese Christian who had murdered a Muslim and was targeted for bashings by Islamic inmates.

'Yeah, I'm a Muslim,' Atkinson said, 'but I had nothing to do with it. I cracked him because he was bragging about what he'd done.'

Atkinson said Halloun, who'd failed to throw a punch, sobbed during the bashing.

'He was just saying he was sorry for what he'd done – shit like that. He was crying like a little bitch.'

And soon, another inmate in the cage was crying too.

'A guy started waving to the officers,' Atkinson said. 'He'd dogged me. He ended up having to go to protection too. He actually pissed and shat his pants while I was belting

Halloun. They had to change his clothes before they took him off to be looked up with the Dogs.'

Is Atkinson just talking tough? *Nope.* He *is* tough. During our series of interviews, I found him to be honest, humble . . . even a good bloke.

Guards have backed him up, too.

'His account is accurate,' confirmed a current Goulburn officer, who asked to remain anonymous. 'It happened in a holding cage at the back of the visits centre. And he gave [Halloun] an absolute hiding. He's a tough boy and very good with his hands. And it was a pretty vicious beating he gave him, stomping the scum and everything. You'd be surprised how much damage can be done in such a short amount of time.'

The Goulburn officer also confirmed the 'Dog', the guy who called on guards to stop the attack, was sent to the 'Dog-yard' following the attack. He too was now fearing for his life.

'It's certainly a big deal calling guards in to an incident between inmates,' the officer continued. 'Especially when they're dobbing on such a heavy-hitter like Goldie. If you lag on a bloke like him, then you'd definitely get clipped if you didn't go into protection. That bloke signed on for protection as soon as he was let out.'

The officer claimed that there was no conspiracy involved in the incident. Halloun had not been put in the yard to be bashed by Goldie – to either extract a charge from the hardman or to have a hated killer killed.

'It was simply a stuff-up,' the senior corrections officer continued. 'The bloke who'd put Halloun into that yard was a pretty inexperienced officer who hadn't spent much time, if any, in the visiting section.

'I think he was only there temporarily to relieve somebody else. That section is usually supervised by permanent visit staff who have intimate knowledge of that section and the type of things that go on. But this bloke didn't have a clue.'

As a protection inmate, Halloun was supposed to be put in a holding cell of his own.

'It was a pretty big mistake,' the officer continued. 'Tony was being kept down in the back of the jail at the MPU [Metropolitan Protection Unit]. He should have never come in contact with anyone other than a fellow protection inmate.'

All the guards – well, except maybe one – knew Halloun needed to be protected more than most.

'They just wanted to get him because of his crime,' the officer said. 'It was on the news a lot and in all the papers. Everyone in the prison system knew he had killed that old lady. He killed her in her house because she caught him robbing the place. She was an innocent lady. An elderly lady, too, and that sort of thing is not on. There is still a prison code, and people like him are to be got because of his offence.

'Everyone in Goulburn, where all the high-profile crims go, watch TV. They watch the news and they know about blokes like Halloun, and they will find out when they're coming in.'

And they'll put out the word – *an order to kill* . . .

'They will start talking about getting blokes like this as

soon as they know they're coming,' said the officer. 'And then they will just wait for their opportunity. No matter how much you try to protect them, down the track, somewhere along the line, they will eventually find a way to gain access to these blokes.

'We've even had cases where inmates have signed on for protection so they can go in and get another protection inmate. They will sign off on a jail protection order saying they are "at threat", when really they just want to go into the protection area to get at a Dog and make a name for themselves. They just play the game.'

And prisoners are patient. With nothing but time on their hands, they are prepared to wait, wait and wait some more . . .

'They play that game for a while,' he continued. 'Sometimes for two or three years. They wait that long to be put in protection if they really want to go after somebody.'

As for Halloun . . . well, nobody even knew where he was. Not until Goldie grabbed him and almost beat him to death.

'People might have wanted to get him,' another unnamed officer said, 'but to be honest, they didn't even know where he was held.'

Halloun suffered serious injuries in the attack, which lasted no more than 11 seconds.

'I spoke to an officer who took Halloun to hospital,' the officer continued. 'He had a fractured eye, a broken nose socket and a suspected broken jaw. He got a real touch-up, and they had to take him to an eye specialist in Sydney after his initial trip to the hospital.

'He told them he had no idea why this guy had belted him. He said the other guy was just a thug. He knew who Atkinson was, and he carried on about him being a hitman. But to most inmates who know Atkinson, that wasn't a surprise. He's pretty high-profile and has been involved with some heavy dudes.'

Halloun is now under heavy protection. Only the men who guard him know where he is. And they are under strict instructions not to tell.

'He's not at Goulburn anymore,' said another Goulburn guard.

'They could be hiding him in the MPU, but as far as I know he's been moved somewhere else. He's probably being shuffled between jails so nobody can get a fix on him. He's one of those guys who has to be moved around because he's going to get flogged wherever he goes. I couldn't even count the number of blokes who've told me they want to get him, but nobody knows where to find him.'

As for Goldie?

'Well, yeah,' the guard said. 'He's pretty hard. He's not a bloke you want to fuck with.'

But a few in Goulburn did, and they paid the price. More on that later. First, let's find out more about Goldie and why he was classified an Extreme High Risk prisoner in Australia's most murderous jail.

Guns and Gold Teeth

An armed battalion of police burst through the door.

'This is a raid,' they yelled. 'Don't move.'

Atkinson – nicknamed 'Goldie' because of his top row of gold teeth, one embedded with a diamond – complied.

The 185cm man, a heavily tattooed body builder bulging with muscle, stood still as the police went about trashing his Rosehill home. Guns drawn, the men in bulletproof vests scurried through every room. Goldie could do little except wait to see if they would find his stash.

And find it they did.

What's this, hey? Lie face-down on the ground and put your hands behind your back.

The boys in blue discovered more than they expected when they raided the house on Penelope Lucas Lane. At first they found drugs, a gun and a bulletproof vest. The weapon? A .22-calibre Ruger self-loading pistol with a silencer was found in a kitchen cupboard. The drugs? 9.3 grams of heroin with a street value of up to $4,000 and 12 vials of assorted steroids, no doubt for personal use.

A holster and ammunition were found under his bed. The bulletproof vest was in his wardrobe.

More concerning than the drugs and guns was what they found in a black backpack in Atkinson's bedroom . . . It contained two photographs of a man named John Macris, an address, two car registration numbers, a loaded .45-calibre semi-automatic pistol and a New South Wales police badge.

Police claim they stormed Atkinson's home on 29 September 2009 to stop Goldie from murdering Macris in a contract killing. Macris, according to police, was about to be 'taken out' because of suspicions he'd tried to kill a member of the infamous Ibrahim family in a drive-by shooting.

Fadi Ibrahim, the second youngest of four brothers, was shot five times outside his Castle Cove home in Sydney's north as he sat in his black Lamborghini on 5 June 2009. He was hit in the arm, chest and stomach while his girlfriend, sitting beside him, suffered a leg wound during the ambush.

Fadi, an associate of the bikie club Notorious and brother of convicted criminals Sam and Michael Ibrahim – and Kings Cross tsar John – was left in a coma for three weeks following the shooting. He was lucky to survive. And so was Marcis, whom Fadi and Michael suspected of being the gunman.

An Ibrahim associate told the *Sunday Telegraph* that it was the police who told the Ibrahims that Macris was responsible for the shooting. Marcis, a 37-year-old restaurateur at the time of the incident, had an interest in an Oxford Street nightclub with his brother John. Police claimed they foiled a hit on Macris after intercepting more than 7,000 calls between Fadi, Michael and would be gunman Goldie Atkinson. Police began listening to the calls between the trio after Goldie visited Michael in prison, where he was serving time for manslaughter.

Police said that information obtained from the phone taps revealed Fadi had delivered photos of the target to Atkinson. Goldie is alleged to have called Michael on a mobile phone that had been smuggled into prison. Goldie told him he was 'going shopping soon' and that he would be very happy with the 'purchase'.

Police swooped on Atkinson soon after the call, believing 'shopping' was code for buying a gun, and an attempt would be made on Macris's life. Following the 9am raid, Goldie was taken to Parramatta Police Station and charged with one count of conspiracy to murder and a series of firearm and drug charges. Prosecutor Eric Balodis accused Fadi, Michael and Atkinson of conspiring to murder Macris between 5 July and 24 September 2009.

'Michael suspected that John Macris was behind the shooting of Fadi,' Mr. Balodis said. 'The evidence will reveal he actively engaged in a plan of retaliation with the intention of having him killed.'

A former associate, who can only be known as 'W1', said he discussed hiring a hitman with Michael and that the going rate was '$300,000'. He alleged that Michael said he had a guy who would do it for $100,000.

'He looked at me and mouthed "Goldie",' W1 said.

Segregated in Solitary at Silverwater
Goldie was locked up in segregation at Silverwater's MRRC throughout the duration of his trial. He would not see another soul, apart for the officers who bought him his food, for three years. The only exception was when he was in court or under heavy guard escort during visits.

It's pretty safe to say he was held in segro illegally. Whatever happened to 'innocent until proven guilty'?

'I had a reputation when I went in,' Atkinson said. 'The police were saying I was a contract killer and I had to be put in segregation [while on remand] to stop it from happening again. It was just really weird shit. The police were the ones who had built my reputation. Before they went spreading shit rumours about me being a hitman, I was just a young bloke from Newcastle. Next, I'm in jail with all these bullshit rumours going around. I think people were giving them information about me to get themselves out of trouble.'

Atkinson, who was first convicted of robbery for stealing $70 to buy cannabis when he was 18, was locked up in a 4 metre by 3 metre cage for up to 22 hours a day.

'I would rather be locked away in [Goulburn's] Supermax than stuck in segregation at Silverwater,' Atkinson said. 'In Supermax you get a decent yard, your own kitchen, and you can associate with other people. It gets pretty fucked up when you don't even have anyone to talk to. At Silverwater, where I stayed for three years, all I had aside from my shitty cell was a little cage at the back.'

Atkinson described a typical day in segregation at the prison, dubbed by a former police minister as 'Hotel Silverwater'.

'The guards come in and do a head check at 6am,' Atkinson recalled, 'which is basically to make sure you haven't committed suicide. And then you get your breakfast.'

Inmates are given a small bag of cereal, a sachet of coffee and a 300ml carton of milk.

'They just kick your door open and shove it in like you're a dog. You don't go and eat in a dining hall or anything like that. You just sit there eating the shit food on your own.'

The boredom is not broken, but it may be blunted when they are allowed out into a yard.

'They open up the back door to let a bit of fresh air in,' Atkinson said. 'And that back door leads out to a bit of a cage. That is your only exercise yard. It would probably be 2 metres by 1 metre.'

Atkinson would be escorted from his cell to use the phone.

'Sometimes you would get to make calls,' he said. 'You would ask them if you could make phone calls, and you'd consider it a good day if you got one. The calls, speaking to your family or lawyer or whatever, was the only part of the day you would really look forward to.'

Atkinson said he never had a TV or radio in his cell.

'Sometimes you got books and newspapers,' Atkinson said. 'But that all depends on who you are and what your privilege level was. I'd had nothing for a while. Certainly not a thing during my first couple of weeks in that hell hole.'

Atkinson claimed the only thing that got him through his three-year segregation stretch was exercise – the giant maintained his monstrous musculature with a rigorous work-out regimen.

'I got through it by doing exercise,' Atkinson said. 'I trained every day. If I didn't do some sort of cardio, then I would do 50 push-ups, 50 sit-ups, 50 squats, and then mountain climbers – for ten sets each. I would do that twice a day – once in the morning and once at night.'

Pumping out push-ups and pull-ups was the only thing that kept him sane.

'It's ridiculous that they can throw you into segregation before you've even been convicted of anything,' Atkinson said. 'They'll throw you in segro for anything these days. If they suspect you're in a gang or that you associate with one, then you're in. If they *think* you're going to get someone, then you're in too. They don't even need proof.'

Atkinson said a judge recommended he be taken out of segregation following a series of complaints. But the direction was ignored by corrections officials.

'They were told to take me out,' Goldie said. 'The judge said it was doing me more harm than good and would only make me worse. But they didn't act on that for at least a year. They do whatever they want in there.'

Atkinson was stunned that some inmates chose to live in a segregation cell at Silverwater, when he was forced to do it is a punishment.

'A lot of people are just in there hiding,' Atkinson said. 'They would be better off taking their chances and fronting up to whatever it is they've done. Because, really, you get nothing in there and they make life as tough as possible for you. The whole process is just pathetic. Trying to get something you need is pretty much impossible because the application process is just a joke.'

Atkinson vented whenever he got the chance.

'I didn't sit back and cop nothing,' he said. 'Even though I was in segro for three years I didn't co-operate. If anyone gave me shit, then I went on with it. I would never back down.'

Atkinson was never convicted on the conspiracy to murder charge.

'I was found not guilty. The only thing I really went down for is the guns, and what I'd done in jail for the Tony Halloun matter.'

A current serving guard agreed that segregation at Silverwater is worse than Supermax at Goulburn. 'In Silverwater, the high-risk guys go to a wing called Darcy 4. It's a long, thin corridor separated in the middle by an office. It's similar to the HRMU [High-Risk Management Unit] but worse. It's just a row of 6 metre by 4 metre cells with a door. At the back of it you have a cage area with a bit of concrete, like a little jail within a jail. If people can't comply, that's where they're sent.

'It's worse to live there than Supermax. Life in the HRMU is gold. It's brand new, modern, and the staff are all good. You're looked after. You have microwaves, access to TVs and pretty much any modern convenience, if you behave.

'In Darcy, they have nothing. Darcy is just for remand. The worst go there as long as they don't have a double-A rating [an inmate charged with a terror-related crime]. Double-A ratings go straight to Supermax, even if they are on remand.'

The officer said inmates are kept in Darcy 4 to keep costs down for the department during the court process.

'The reason why they're kept there is because Silverwater is much closer to the courts. Imagine driving someone from Goulburn every day to attend court for a case that might go on for nine months. It's just not practical. It would cost a fortune to have all the armed escorts. Some of these guys, the real bad dudes, have a small army escorting them whenever they are taken outside the walls of a jail. There are about 1,300 inmates at Silverwater, and they're farmed out [to other jails] as soon as their court cases are done. They are placed and classified.'

Brett Collins, a former inmate turned academic, argues that authorities are using a loophole to put inmates into segregation without cause. Collins was locked up in several prisons, including Long Bay Jail and Grafton, and was famous for protesting when he was an inmate. He famously sat on a roof at Long Bay Jail for four days. He was one of only a few prisoners to be labelled an 'intractable'.

'We had a big issue with segregation at Lithgow a couple of years ago,' said Collins, who now heads an inmate activist group called Justice Action. 'Some [Indigenous] inmates said they hadn't done anything wrong, but they had been put in a so-called "program", which included being placed in a segregation cell. This program meant that they were given nothing. Basically it was a way to get around the law and put them in segregation without any recourse.'

Collins explained that there is a process that allows prisoners to appeal and challenge their segregation sentence.

Or there should be . . .

'We took this matter up with the commissioner [Peter Severin]. We looked carefully at the issue of whether or not they have the right to take things away from inmates and put them in solitary.

'There is a hierarchy of ways in which it can happen. Number one, you can be charged with offences, then you have a right of appeal before things are taken away.

'The second way is that you can be placed in segregation according to a section of the act. And after two weeks they need permission from the commissioner to extend the segregation further. It's very carefully stated and the rules are clear. You have the right to be considered by the Serious Offenders Review Council [SORC].

'The third way is a separate issue and the one we're looking at. In another section of the act they say you can be separated and put in a program. They don't regard it as a punishment; rather, it's a way of changing the behaviour. They can hold you there indefinitely and it's totally arbitrary as well.'

Atkinson's segregation cell-hell ended when he was sent to Goulburn to serve the remainder of his sentence for drug and firearm offences.

Fights and Phones

'Get off the fucking phone!' Goldie screamed. 'How many calls do you need to make?'

Atkinson stood and stewed.

Seriously? How long do I have to stand here and wait for this spinner?

And then he got angry.

'Come on, sir, this bloke is making call after call,' he pleaded to the officer. 'I need to use the phone too.'

The officer nodded. 'You'll get your turn.'

He would . . . but not for a while.

'[The officer] just kept letting this one bloke use the phone,' Goldie recalled. 'And this bloke was continually phoning the [New South Wales] ombudsman. When you ring the ombudsman, you don't have to pay for phone calls.'

With no need for coins, the inmate picked up the phone, dialled, waited . . . and then hung up.

Then he did it again and again and again . . .

'He kept on ringing,' Atkinson said. 'He would get through, complain about some shit, and then do it all again.'

Atkinson was no longer angry. *He was furious.*

'That's *enough!*' he shouted. 'For fuck's sake!'

Finally, the guard agreed and ended the inmate's telethon.

Your turn, Atkinson. Go for it.

Goldie picked up the handset, inserted his phone card and dialled some digits.

'I'd just gotten through to my mum,' Atkinson said, before hearing the guard call out: 'That's it. Time's up. Back to your cell.'

'I told him to fuck off, because it was disrespectful. I had waited and waited, and when my turn came he gave me 30 seconds.'

Atkinson, all gold teeth and Gold's Gym, snarled.

'You want to have a go?' the guard enquired. 'You reckon you can get it over me?'

Atkinson nodded.

Of course he could. He knew he could.

106

The guard led the inmate back to his cell, not a camera in site . . .

Crack!

The guard hit first.

Crack! Crack!

Now Atkinson.

'I was getting it over him,' Atkinson said. 'I was surprised he even went through with it, but we were fighting – one-on-one – and I started hurting him.' And that's when the reinforcements arrived. 'His mates came in as soon as I started to get on top. I didn't even know they were there until they were all over me.'

A guard rushed in . . . quickly followed by another.

'Soon there was a whole squad in there. And they gave it to me.'

With three officers now on his back, the handcuffs coming out and about to go on, and the beating still in full force, Atkinson went momentarily mad.

'I was in a rage,' he said. 'I was getting flogged and I just wanted to kill those blokes. I had a shiv under my pillow, so I decided I was going to stab the cunts. That was the only way I was going to win. I was seriously that mad – I wanted to kill them, and in my mind I thought I would.'

Atkinson went for the shiv. 'It was made from spikes in the bed. I'd wrapped it up with a bit of cloth, or something like that.'

Goldie reached and was able to pull the pillow off. But the shiv? It was out of reach. An officer saw the weapon and grabbed it.

No stabbing or slashing for you today, mate.

The handcuffs went on and the beating continued – only harder and heavier, now that they knew Goldie was prepared to kill.

Atkinson said guards regularly beat inmates. 'The screws still do it. Most of the time they'll wait until you're handcuffed, and then they'll lay in. Silverwater is a lot worse than Goulburn – it's renown for it. [The MRRC] got so many complaints, that officers were banned by the ombudsman from working in certain sections of the jail. A lot were not allowed in the segregation unit because there were no cameras in that wing. The guards with a history of violence had to work in areas that were monitored by cameras.'

Atkinson was asked if he wanted to lay charges for the fight when he was found, battered and bruised. He said no, of course. In return, he was not charged for fighting, but he was charged and punished for the shiv.

'They should show some backbone and keep it one-on-one or not start it up at all.'

Brothers in Strife

'Can you slap him once in the face?' asked Bassam Hamzy, the Brothers 4 Life co-founder, speaking on the mobile phone that had been smuggled into Lithgow Jail by way of arse. You know, that same phone he famously used to make an average of 460 calls a day from his maximum-security prison cell? The one he used to run his drug empire, despite being locked up for life?

'I've already done it, cuz,' said the voice on the other end of the line. 'I've got blood everywhere, mate.'

He issued another command during another call. 'Put something in his mouth. Tie his mouth up so he can't scream. He's lucky I don't put a bullet in his head. If I ever have to come up there again, I'm gonna cut all his fingers off. Next time I'll take his ears and make them into a necklace.'

In a startling admission, Goldie Atkinson has confirmed that he was the mystery man on the other end of the line for the infamous 'ear-severing call'. In fact, Atkinson said he was the guy who took most of the 19,000 calls made by Hamzy over a six-week period in 2008.

'But if you read all the transcripts,' Atkinson said, 'most of that stuff is just absolute shit.'

Police alleged that Hamzy orchestrated the kidnapping of John Baroutas in Adelaide on 5 June 2008 after 'an associate' told him the man owed him money. Court documents revealed that Hamzy was on the phone as two men stormed into Baroutas's house and asked the victim, 'Where's my money?'

Atkinson admits he was one of the men described as 'cronies' sent to do the notorious inmate's 'dirty work'.

'They got us in Adelaide, and I was in the house. That was true. But all the things they said happened were just bullshit.'

Atkinson said he was stringing Hamzy along, telling him he was cutting, punching and slapping . . .

'But I wasn't hurting him at all,' Atkinson continued. 'I was just telling Bas what he wanted to hear. He was tripping out and talking shit. We had the phone on loudspeaker and we were playing along. Bas was saying, "Cut his ear off, bash him, flog him," and I was kind of winking at [Baroutas], saying, *Go with it mate*.

'We both got charged for the matter, but there was never a conviction because nothing happened. No witness ever came forward. There was no blood [at the scene]. No complaint was ever made.'

Goldie Atkinson was a founding member of Brothers 4 Life and was 'best mates' with Hamzy before the pair fell out over the alleged kidnapping in Adelaide.

'We started BFL together,' Atkinson said, 'and we were very close. It was just meant to be a brotherhood when it started. We all had a basic belief in Islam and we all stuck together. We were unlike other bikie gangs – we wanted to be nothing like bikies.

'We were brothers. We were to do what we thought was right by each other without having to go high up to a leader or provide proof.'

But Atkinson said he soon grew tired of the 'gang' he helped create.

'It just became young blokes trying to get a name for themselves,' Atkinson said. 'That's all it was – the complete *opposite* of what it was supposed to be. The BFL members started killing their own family for money and drugs, and that's just fucked up. I didn't want to be a part of that.'

Atkinson's first major crime involved meat cleavers, pistols, a horse and a 'horse's hoof'.

'I was just out of jail,' Atkinson said. 'And part of my parole conditions were that I had to go and live in this rehabilitation house. I wasn't allowed to return to Newcastle and the court ordered me to stay in the house with a bloke who was to be my "psych", and take prescription medicine. It knocked me out at night for about a week, but after that it wasn't as effective. It wasn't working as well.'

Soon the doctor was asking Goldie for some help.

'He knew I was a bit of a fighter,' Atkinson said. 'He knew from the courts that I had a history of street crime, and most of it was for assaults and fighting. I'd never really done anything serious until then. It was just punching on, alcohol and drugs. Anyway, he approached me with some pictures.'

This is my horse. Look at him? See how sick he is? We need to go and get him back. They're not taking care of him.

'He reckoned this horse was worth about $25K,' Goldie continued. 'And he said we needed to go and take it back or it would die. It was his horse, he had given it up, and now he wanted it back.'

So Atkinson got his boys – a couple of former 'coeys' – and they put two meat cleavers and two pistols in the car. Then they went for a drive, on a mission to reclaim the sick horse.

'We got there and they were all carrying on like idiots,' Atkinson said, recalling the men waving cleavers and pistols, shouting and screaming. 'No one had cut the phone line; it was very unprofessional. The bloke refused to say where the horse was.'

111

So Goldie walked up and gave him until the count of three.

'Then I knocked him out. He wouldn't tell me so I whacked him.'

Atkinson waited until his victim regained consciousness, hopefully now a bit more willing to talk.

'I asked him again,' Atkinson said. 'I was about to [hit him] again but a neighbour came out, saying he had called the cops.'

So they took off.

'Halfway home we got picked up by the cops,' Goldie said. 'I copped the rap, along with another bloke. I ended up getting about five months, I think. I could've rolled on the old bloke for being a fraud and whatever, but I didn't, so I ended up getting a fair whack.'

But it could have been worse.

'Apparently I had been charged with "horse rustling". The judge looked at me when I was in court and asked me if I knew that it was still a hanging offence. The law hadn't been changed or used since back in Ned Kelly's days. Thankfully, they got me with just affray and assault instead.'

Atkinson has regrets – not about bashing the granny-murdering grub, but about the gang he helped create. Or at least, what it became.

'I was a bit gullible to be honest,' Atkinson said. 'I thought they were my brothers and I went along with the things they did. I was just young and thought that if I did all these things for them then they would do things for me. I thought it was a family and that we were there to look after each other. It ended up being the opposite. All the killings, the back-stabbing . . . It just turned to shit.'

Brothers 4 Life is officially no longer a gang, according to authorities anyway.

'It's pretty much over,' Atkinson said, 'but there are still guys out there who use the name. There are two different chapters now. There's an Afghanistan-based one and there's another with Lebanese boys. They don't get on and are fighting [on the street and in prison].'

Atkinson was eventually shipped out of Goulburn in a 'prisoner swap' and sent on to Nowra.

'As I said, I didn't take any shit,' Goldie continued. 'And I was constantly threatened with Supermax. But that wasn't something I was worried about, and they knew it. I wasn't scared one bit of Supermax. Whenever they threatened me, I would say, "Are you here to take me there now?" They would say no, and then I would tell them to fuck off. All my mates were in Supermax, so why wouldn't I want to go there? Compared to where I was, Supermax was heaps better. But the thing was Mick [Ibrahim] was there, and they didn't want me associating with him. They were never going to put me in with him.

'Anyway, I had heaps more blues, and they ended up asking me if I wanted to go back into "segro" and go through all that shit again – or I could move to another jail. They offered me a prisoner exchange. I accepted and was moved to Nowra.'

Atkinson was released from Nowra prison after serving six years of his maximum nine-year sentence. The infamous inmate has turned his back on crime and now lives on the north coast of New South Wales.

Goldie is a family man, caring not for crime, guns or drugs, but only for his daughter and wife. He is one of a few who left prison a better man, in spite of the system's best efforts to break him.

Goldie's bid to go straight has not been made easy by the police, and by those who refuse to believe a man with his extensive criminal record can walk away from a life of ill-gotten gains.

Shortly after concluding a series interviews for this book, Atkinson was arrested following a targeted swoop in March when he was caught with over $100,000 in cash. It was alleged the cash was from the proceeds of crime, and the former enforcer was sent back to Silverwater for a short stint. Goldie was released on bail and claims to have a legitimate explanation for the large amount of money. He expects the charges to be dropped soon.

Another blow was to come.

Atkinson revealed his plan to become a UFC fighter in an interview with the *Sunday Telegraph* on 10 April. He was scheduled to fight in his first professional bout on 7 May against a martial arts expert in a 90kg battle at Liverpool. He spoke about professional fighting saving him from his life of crime.

'The sport has changed my life,' Atkinson said. 'It has taught me to control my aggression and anger. I have really been working hard to turn my life around, and I want to be here for my wife and daughter.'

I went along to one of Atkinson's training sessions.

With his bulging muscles, gold teeth and fearsome gaze, Atkinson smashed pads, walloped the heavy bag and bounced around like a fighter in his prime. He had been training for his debut fight for at least six months and was determined to forge a career as a professional Mixed Martial Arts fighter.

'I've had a lot of trouble getting this first fight,' Atkinson said. 'A lot of people agree but then pull out when they Google me and see some of the things I've done. It's been a difficult road but this is the first step. I now have a chance to show that I deserve this and show everyone what I can do.'

Goldie's dream was crushed just a few days after the article was published.

'Liverpool police stepped in and banned the event,' Atkinson told me. 'They said that the fight would pose a public risk and there was a threat of an attack at the event.'

The Australian Combat Sports Authority then refused to issue Atkinson with a fighter's licence.

'They said I was not a proper person to hold a licence because of my criminal record. I've just had to cop it. I can't be a fighter until this is sorted out. It has shattered me and the whole situation is just fucked. This is what I've been working towards, and I don't know what I can do. This is the sort of shit I've to go through.

'I have to start looking at new things. Maybe I'll start a gym or look at owning a protein shop. I still want to be around the sport. I'm not going to give up.'

Atkinson feels hard done by, with numerous fighters in Australia forging a career in various combat sports despite sporting criminal records. Some of Australia's most successful boxers, both past and present, have serious criminal histories.

'That's the price I pay for my past,' Atkinson said. 'I have to cop it and move on.'

6

[CRAIG'S] FIELD OF [BROKEN] DREAMS

Cessnock Maximum-Security, Grafton and the MRRC

Visits

An officer waves at me and shakes his head. 'Not that one, mate.'

I look down.

'Oh,' I say and sheepishly slide over to the silver stool, nodding.

'Yeah, red is for them,' he continues.

I wink and whisper, 'Thanks, mate.'

I put the vending-machine haul down on the table: a two-foot-high steel circle surrounded by three silver stools, *and a red one.*

Does he even eat this shit? He's an athlete – or at least he was?

Before being fingerprinted (*for the second time*) and let through yet another pair of submarine-like metal doors, I spend the maximum twenty-dollar limit (*coins only*) on a packet of Allen's Party Mix lollies, a can of Coke, a bottle of water, a bag of Maltesers and a packet of sea salt-flavoured Kettle chips.

Why didn't they tell me what he likes? They told me to bring the coins, they told me about the machines, but they didn't give me their standard line before I was let in: 'Make your choice before entering the visit – you will not be allowed back out under any circumstances.'

The can, the bottle and the bag, chock-full of *guesses*, swamp the tiny table. The brightly coloured lolly wrappings are the only signs of life in this white-walled room, all steel chairs and sad faces.

It is sterile and silent. I want to say something to the man who told me not to sit on the red stool, something like, *Hey, who are you waiting for? What's he in for?* But I'm not sure if talking is allowed, or if the questions are appropriate.

So I sit and wait . . .

Ten minutes pass and I am still alone at my table.

Where is he?

There are 17 other people in the room and, like me, they sit silently on silver stools, looking at tables topped with colourful cans and candy.

The red chairs remain empty . . .

Crescendo!

'Ali!' a woman in a hijab says. 'Ali, Ali, as-Salāmu alaykum.'

Peace be with you. I understand because I grew up in

Bankstown. I was one of four kids in Year Six who had a square sandwich instead of a tabouli-filled cylindrical wrap.

He sits, the first arse – aside from my momentarily misplaced one – to rest on red.

The room is now *pianissimo* – the young man of Middle Eastern descent speaks softly to his . . . *mother?* He's a skinny, unshaven kid, no more then 20, and he smiles as he whispers, the sound of bursting lolly bags and crunching chips louder than their conversation.

Crescendo!

Another man in a white jumpsuit emerges from the void and the volume is turned up. Zip-ties on his wrists, ankles and neck, this beefy man first hugs a woman (*his wife?*) and then a little girl (*his daughter?*).

One by one, the inmates shuffle out in their Dunlop Volleys (velcro straps, of course) and zip-tied jumpsuits.

Louder! Forte!

The room is almost full. Every red chair now accommodates a bum – except one.

'Who you waiting for, buddy?' an officer interrupts.

Shit! Does he know who I am? Does he know about my two other jail books?

'Fieldsy,' I shoot. 'Craig Field.'

The guard nods and wanders back to his aircraft-controller-like box filled with CCTV screens, computers and other watchful guards.

Finally he enters.

'Phelpsy?' He not so much asks but confidently assumes it's me.

How does he know what I look like? Ah. Last empty red chair . . .

'Fieldsy,' I declare, standing up and extending my right hand. 'How are you?'

I wait for him to say, *'How the fuck do you think I am?'*

'Yeah good, mate,' he replies. 'Can't complain.'

He sits on a *silver* stool.

'Ah,' he says, noting my shock. 'What are they going to do?'

I point towards the junk food. 'Mate, I'm not even sure you eat this shit. I just grabbed a bit of everything in case.'

He smiles.

'Thanks, mate,' he says, already ripping into the bag of chips.

'Not usually, but on days like this? Well . . . I'll eat it all. We don't get any of this stuff. The food in here is pretty plain. You don't know how much stuff like this means to me. Thanks.'

He shakes my hand again.

'I bought you socks,' I say. 'A three-pack of Nikes. They're the low-cut ones. I hope they're okay. I didn't know if you blokes wear high socks or anklets?'

He nods before shaking my hand again.

'Serious?' he says. 'Mate, that is so kind. They're perfect. Thank you.'

I tell him I left them with the officer at the front door – the one who fingerprinted me, scanned my eyes and took a copy of my licence. He also issued me a receipt for the socks after checking that there were no drugs or shivs concealed in a toe end.

'I'll get 'em mate,' he says. 'As long as they're white.'

They were. I booked the visit three days before and, while on hold for five minutes, the message was clear: 'The only thing you can bring as a gift is socks – white. Undies, not boxers – white. You can also bring thermals – white – but only if they are clearly marked with the word "thermal" either on the packaging, the item or the receipt.'

I smile. 'I tried to get you thermals, but I couldn't find any in white.'

Craig gives me a friendly shove. 'It's 42 degrees today – I'll take the socks.'

I give him a little slap on the shoulder as he shovels down snakes. I immediately like this bloke. Yep . . . this Bulldog from Bankstown likes this Rabbitoh from Redfern.

How could I not?

Even though I supported and had been lucky enough to have played Rugby League in the lower grades for the Canterbury-Bankstown Bulldogs, the team that *hates* every NRL team Craig Field played for – South Sydney, Manly and the Wests Tigers – here I am sitting next to the bloke.

I'm thinking it, so I might as well say it.

'Mate, how does a guy who was earning $600,000 a year – a bloke who played 183 first-grade games – end up here, thanking some journo he's never met for a packet of snakes and some socks?'

This is the question I put to Craig Field – the NRL legend sentenced to ten years for manslaughter – as we sit in the maximum-security visits section of Cessnock Correctional Centre.

And the following is his story, the former Rugby League star opening up about his crime and time in one of Australia's toughest prisons, in his one and only interview . . .

A Pub and a Punch
15 July 2012

On most Sundays you could find the ex-footy star at the Kingscliff Beach Hotel, having a beer and placing a bet, talking sport with friends, but usually not until the late afternoon. That day was different – *and eventually deadly* – with Fieldsy rocking up at about 11am so he could watch a former player box.

'I went there a bit earlier than usual,' Field recalls, settling into the silver seat. 'The Mundine fight was on and the pub was showing it live on the big screen. I was there with a mate from footy, having a quiet beer and a punt, watching the fight.'

Field was drinking with Shaun Fathers, who they all called 'Feathers'. He had met the local after moving to the stunning coastal town of Kingscliff, located just south of Tweed Heads in northern New South Wales, in 2010 to continue his fading-fast footy career.

Field was 37 when he signed on to play two years with the Cudgen Hornets, the former Rabbitoh, Sea Eagle and Tiger almost ready to call it quits. Having completed his last NRL game in 2001, he first played and then captain-coached in France before heading to Wagga Wagga to do the same.

Field – a Rugby League journeyman – felt like he was finally home.

'Things were going so well,' he says. 'I went up there to play and then coach, and it was just a beautiful place. I lost everything when I finished up with the Wests Tigers. I didn't have a cent. I got caught up with someone who gave me some real bad investment advice, and I ended up losing all the properties I owned and all my cash. Anyway, I put that behind me and got on with it, and eventually I ended up in Kingscliff.'

Field earned a bit of money from the Hornets, first to play and then to coach. He still had enough lightning in his passes, thunder in his kicks and wind behind his dashes and darts to push him through holes. The No.7 was still good enough to be a star in the country competition, but Field knew he couldn't play forever.

'I was really lucky that I had a trade,' Field continues. 'I'm a qualified electrician, and while I was playing up there I set up a business and started working full-time.'

And business was good.

'I had about five big contracts. I had a couple of pubs, the leagues club and some other businesses that I serviced exclusively. I was finally putting my life back together after having a pretty hard time when footy finished up.'

So Field was set. Family of five firmly by his side, he had begun a new life by the beach.

If only he hadn't gone to the pub . . .

The real fights started when the main event ended, Anthony Mundine dropping Bronco McKart in the seventh to win his first bout in America. While Field's former footy rival, in the flush of victory, was on the screen challenging champion Floyd Mayweather Jr to a fight, Field was trying to stop one in the pub.

A bloke called Mark Frost had just made a remark about the manager Geoff Wallis's recently deceased baby – and the publican was rightfully raging.

'Frosty and the manager were having some sort of argument,' Field says. 'He'd probably had too much to drink, but he took it way too far by making a comment about the manager having a stillborn baby.'

The publican rushed towards Frosty, ready to smash in his face. Enter Field.

'Mate,' Field said as he grabbed Wallis and held him back. 'What he said is terrible, but you can't do this. Stop and think. You'll lose your licence if you fight him. It's not worth it.'

The manager came to his senses and Field forced Frosty to apologise.

'I was trying to break up fights all day,' Field recalls. 'Speak to anyone who was there and they'll tell you that I was playing the role of peacemaker. I defused a number of situations that day.'

His mate Feathers soon began bluing with one of Frosty's friends, a woman named Lyn Burger. What happened between the two remains unclear.

'There were some accusations that he had grabbed her around the throat,' Field says. 'But he hadn't done it.'

Feathers, Burger, Field and Frosty all ended up outside.

'I was telling Feathers to cool it. He was angry about the accusations.'

Angry? Feathers had allegedly just thrown a bar chair.

'I was also trying to shut the woman up. Shaun didn't touch her. And she was going off.'

And that is when Kelvin Kane, a 51-year-old local cattle farmer, and friends with both Frosty and Lyn, stepped in.

'He hadn't heard the remark his mate Frosty had said to the manager about the stillborn baby,' Field tells me. 'Anyway, I was sorting out that incident and trying to calm them all down, and he came in not knowing what had been said.'

Field became frustrated. He shouted and pointed, telling Kane to stuff off.

'I just told him to shut his mouth. And I did move towards him in an aggressive manner, but no punches were exchanged.'

Not yet . . .

All had quietened down, according to Field. In fact, about 40 minutes had passed since the heated argument about throats, babies and bar stools.

The former football player was now helping the manager 'move on' the troublesome patrons and 'make sure things didn't get out of hand'.

And that's when the shit hit the fan.

'Shaun ran over and pulled Kane out of the car,' Field says. 'It was Feathers who started the fight. I was actually putting Frosty [later described as a "serial pest" in court] in the car and saying goodnight to him when it all kicked off. I coached his kid and thought everything was okay.'

But it wasn't.

'Feathers dragged him out and started throwing punches. I stood there like everyone else, watching the both of them fight.'

But Field said the fight became unfair.

'Feathers started getting held back by others. And that's not on. I went over to break it up. I wouldn't have gotten involved if I hadn't feared for his safety.'

Or if he knew what would happen next . . .

'I went in and the bloke shaped up to me in a boxing stance,' Field said. 'It was a case of him hitting me or me hitting him. That's the way I saw it.'

So Field hit first.

CRACK!

One punch and Kane went down.

'I saw his hand cocked, and out of fear I threw a punch to the right side of his head,' Field says. 'As soon as my fist hit him, he fell down. He just sort of dropped to a knee and he was down.'

Field backed off immediately.

'I shat myself. I could see he was bleeding and had fallen over. A few people rushed to his aid, and they told me to go home. So I did.'

Kelvin Kane required cardiopulmonary resuscitation when the paramedics arrived. The millionaire cattle farmer was taken to hospital and placed on life support. He died the next day when the machine was turned off. This cause of death was listed as a brain haemorrhage, sustained from a punch to the head or his head hitting the ground.

Field was arrested and charged, first with assault and then murder. A man was dead, and this former football player was now facing life in jail.

Convicting Craig

Justice Elizabeth Fullerton sentenced Field, convicted of manslaughter, to a maximum of ten years in jail. Fullerton said the community demanded 'a general deterrence' for 'unprovoked, uncontrollable, lethal violence'.

Field's family wept as they left the Lismore local court, knowing that the husband and father of five would spend a minimum of seven years and six months behind bars, and they would only get to see him a few times a year.

Field, 42 when sentenced, had been cleared of murder a week before he was found guilty of manslaughter for the one-punch attack.

His defence immediately labelled the sentence 'manifestly excessive'.

And it is hard to disagree.

'It was a fight that I never started,' Field says. 'And one I never wanted to get involved in. I was having a beer at the local pub one minute, and soon I was rushing in to stop my mate from being hurt.

'A kid the other day got three years for throwing a king hit . . . I mean, that was a deadset dog shot. My case was nothing like that, and I get ten. I was involved in a fight, but the judges didn't see it that way, and there isn't much I can do.'

Field is adamant Feathers and Kane were exchanging punches before he intervened.

'Shaun got up there and gave testimony that he didn't throw any punches, and that was enough for the judge to put all the blame on me,' Field said. 'It didn't happen like that, and there were witnesses there who saw them both punching. It was a tragic accident and the result of a fight that occurs in pubs. There is no way in the world it was every bit planned or that I wanted to go and meet this bloke and belt him. There was no malice. I had no ill will towards the gentleman who got hit; I never wanted to hurt him.

'My mate was having a fight and, like most people, I couldn't leave him there to get dropped. I back up my mates. I couldn't let him get bashed and I was trying to stop someone from getting hurt. Unfortunately, a tragic thing happened and a man died.'

Left with Legal Aid to defend him, having lost his Rugby League fortune, Field points to a mistake made by his counsel in his defence: a still-frame photo of Field, captured by the hotel's CCTV, was used as evidence during the trial.

'They used a still photo of me going towards the man, looking angry,' Field says. 'I was in a punching pose. That picture was taken 40 minutes *before* the fight took place, but it was made to look like it happened when the punch was thrown. That evidence was taken out of context because it had happened much earlier. This was never pointed out during the trial, and I'm not sure why. I'm not denying that I went towards the guy when the still photo was taken, but that was a *separate* time. I was telling his mate Frosty off for making that remark. Then I motioned to Kane to piss off when he came in. I'm sure he wouldn't have even gotten involved in the way he did if he knew what had gone on.'

Witnesses also gave inconsistent evidence, but the NSW Court of Criminal Appeal upheld Field's maximum ten-year sentence. According to the three-judge appeal panel, 'There was undoubtedly some inconsistencies in and between the witnesses' evidence, such as what colour clothing Mr Kane's hitter was observed to be wearing, whether Mr Kane was hit on the left or right side of his head, and how Mr Kane fell.

'However . . . such inconsistencies are to be expected, particularly in a case such as the present, where those observing the altercation from beyond the car park encountered issues of distance and lighting, and for all witnesses a rapid unfolding of traumatic events.

'The inconsistencies do not, in my view, give rise to any doubt about whether it was the applicant's punch that the witnesses were describing as they all referred to Mr Kane's immediate collapse.'

Field says the 'issues of distance and lighting' did not stop the evidence that led to his conviction from being accepted.

'A lady gave a statement in which she said she saw the incident from a unit block across from the car park. The measurements from the police machine was 52 metres – that's a long way to see in the dark with just one floodlight. Even forensics, when they got to the scene, said it was very poor lighting. Everybody else just said they couldn't see, and it was my honesty that got me convicted. I owned up to the punch. They went off that evidence but then said I was the only one who hit him, because Shaun didn't have the courage to be honest or he was scared of going to jail.'

Field is considering challenging the conviction in the High Court of Australia.

I'm Sorry

While many, including me, feel sorry for Field and think he was excessively punished, Craig is not the victim. No, Kane is the victim . . . along with his family who continues to miss him every single day. Circumstances, court cases and convictions aside, a man was killed, leaving a widow and children behind.

And for that, Field is sorry – eternally sorry.

'They made out that I showed no remorse, but that isn't right,' Field says. 'I think about that gentleman and his family every day. It was the first time I had ever been in trouble with the law, and I didn't know what I should have been saying and shouldn't have been saying. I was worried about every word I said. But of course I feel remorse for the family and their loss. I didn't want to hurt him. And I regret that he did get hurt. I was only thinking about protecting a friend and then protecting myself. The outcome was just tragic. I definitely feel for his family and I'm sorry for what happened. I wish I could take away their pain.'

Field's family are also victims, his loving wife and children forced to fend for themselves while Dad serves his time.

Family and Friends

I look around the room, taking in the sad scene.

There are 14 men in white jumpsuits, sitting on red stools. They are eating candy and chips while they talk, mostly about appeals.

All of the visitors – with the exception of Mr Don't-Sit-On-The-Red-Stool and one other (*a brother?*) – are women and children. I count: there are 13 women and 11 boys and girls; the oldest is a little blonde girl, who looks about four. There are four newborns no older than six months.

I turn to Craig.

'Mate, I really feel for them,' I say as he continues to chug down Coke and crunch on Kettle chips. 'I watched all the kids get searched and fingerprinted before we came in. That little girl,' I point to the blonde, 'was laughing when the guard made her put her hands up and checked her with a metal detector. She thought it was a game.'

Craig nods. 'Yeah, it's hard on the families. You see the same women and kids in here every week. Some off them,' he flicks his head towards a teenage girl with a baby, 'stick by them no matter what. But there isn't a thing you can do for them while stuck in here.'

Craig stops smiling.

'Obviously the hardest thing for me is missing my wife and children,' he says, no longer gulping or snacking. 'I have five kids. The eldest is 23 and the youngest is ten. It's so hard being away from them, and I don't get to see them very often because they live up north – they simply can't afford to keep flying down. They only come in the school holidays, so it's gutting to have to wait so long. But wanting to see them all the time is also a bit selfish. It probably works out a bit better like this, because I don't want my kids growing up in a jail. I want to see them, of course, but I don't want them having to come in here every week and go through all of this.'

He suddenly stops talking as two officers rush towards the back of the room. I'm about to ask what's happening, but I'm pretty sure I already know. *Drugs. Someone has just slipped an inmate some drugs.* The room is silent as the officers pounce. They grab a young Middle Eastern-looking man. Even the kids stop playing, talking and crying – they all turn towards the commotion. The young man is soon dragged out of the room, along with his visitor, the one who gave him the gear.

Crescendo!

Then it's like nothing happened.

'See what I mean?' Field says. 'I don't want them seeing shit like that. To think that's normal.'

He smiles again and resumes his snack-attack. 'But, yeah, it's just the best thing ever when you do get to see them. It's the thing I look forward to the most. But that's just me being selfish. This is all a lot harder on them than it is on me. Ellen has to provide for everyone. It breaks my heart.'

He gives me another friendly slap.

'Even you,' he says, 'a complete stranger 15 minutes before. It's good chatting to you.'

I laugh. 'Mate, you must be sick – no one likes reporters.'

'*Ha!*' he snaps. 'You're okay. But you do learn quickly who your friends are. And it's during times like these you need them the most. I have a good group of guys who come and visit me often. John Elias, Nat Wood, Jim Serdaris, John Hopoate, Josh Stuart, Angelo Ferrelli and Adam Nable come up a lot. Man, do I look forward to that.

'Sitting down and talking about old times, having a laugh and hearing what's going on outside and what everyone is up to is the best. It's so important, and all these guys have come up to see me at least three or four times, Johnny and Nat [former South Sydney teammates] more. To see guys I can relate to is such a good thing, rather than listening to the blokes in here, who are always talking about their cases or girlfriends. Shit like that, you know? It's good to have a laugh rather than just hear blokes complain.

'They also help out my family. They're always in touch with Ellen. The emotional support they give her and my kids means so much to me. They will do anything they can for them. They are my real friends and will be for life. There are so many people who have taken from me over the years, and I thought they were mates, but no . . . As soon as you end up here they don't want a thing to do with you.'

Now, let's go behind the next metal door and into a maximum-security Cessnock prison wing with the former footy player turned inmate . . .

Shitty Cellmates

Field walked into his Cessnock cell after being shipped up from the MRRC following a stint in Grafton, where he was held for the duration of his trial.

Fuck! Is that him? It couldn't be. Could it?

133

The former football player, short but built like a brick shithouse, stared at the Lebanese man sitting on one of the two beds.

Yep. It is. Fuck!

Field dropped his bag of prison-issue possessions, the plastic cutlery inside the canvas rattling as it hit the concrete floor. And then he raised his hands, his palms strangling his fingers as he made a pair of rock-hard fists.

'I couldn't believe it,' Field recalls. 'It was my first night in Cessnock, and here I am standing in front of a guy who was involved in murdering two of my friends and shooting at my mate Nat Wood.'

Field lost two of his footballing friends on 17 July 1998 in a senseless shooting on a Sydney street.

'A few of my mates from footy where having a bit of an argument outside a pub at Five Dock,' Field says. 'It was nothing. Just mates sorting some shit out. Anyway, a car full of Lebanese blokes pulled up and starting shouting shit, egging them on, wanting to see a fight. Then one of them pulled a gun out and started shooting.'

Adam Wright and Michael Hurle died in hospital shortly after the complete stranger gunned them down. Ron Singleton, another of Field's friends, only survived because the gunman had run out of bullets. The shooter had fired a bullet into his leg before raising the gun to his head.

Click!

Nothing.

Notorious Sydney psychopath Michael Kanaan was soon identified as the shooter. The other men in the car with the killer were Shadi Derbas, Bassam Kazzi, an informant known as 'Rossini' and another unidentified man.

Field was now standing in a cell with one of them. 'I just dropped my stuff and thought, *Here we go.*'

Then he remembered the promise he had made to himself. *His vow to never punch anyone again . . .*

'I wasn't sure what to do, but I knew I couldn't be in a cell with him,' Field says.

His vow was tested, but he unclenched his fists and looked at the man. 'You know who I am?' The inmate nodded. 'Well, you have to go. We have to find you another cell right now. This isn't going to work.'

The inmate shook his head. *Nah, man. You got it wrong.*

'He ended up pulling out his case notes,' Field recalls. 'He kept them all on a laptop in his cell. He went through them and proved he had nothing to do with it.'

All right then. Maybe this will work.

Field shook his hand.

'Okay, mate,' he began. 'I have no problem with you. Let's put that behind us and see how we go.'

Field picked up his bag and unpacked.

'We ended up rooming in a two-out cell for three months,' Field said. 'And we even became mates. He was a pretty good bloke, but you can only imagine how we'd both felt when we ended up in a cell together, knowing what had happened in the past.'

Field eventually moved to another cell, where he was soon wishing he was back with one of the men accused of involvement in the murder of his mates . . .

*

SPLAAATTTT!

The liquid shit slapped against the concrete floor and splattered against the steel cell door.

Pppffftttt!

Another explosion of wind and watery shit sprayed the bed, drawers and wall.

'What the fuck?' Field screamed, awoken by the shotgun sound of diarrhoea.

He looked but couldn't see anything in the dark. His nose, however, didn't need time to adjust.

'What's that smell?' he yelled.

No. He couldn't have. Surely not.

Field's pupils widened and he was soon able to cut through the dark.

Yep. He had. Fucking junkie.

'One of my worst experiences with a cellmate involved a bloke on drugs,' Field tells me. 'I was sitting on my bed and saw the bloke pull out a needle. I've done things in the past that I regret, and everyone knows what happened with me at the Tigers. [Field was sacked by the Wests Tigers in 2001 after testing positive for cocaine.] But anyone who knows me will tell you how much I'm against drugs now. And I have always been against needles.'

Yep, a sneaky line of coke with the boys is one thing . . . Shoving a needle into a vein and shooting up smack is another.

'I told him to put it away,' Field says. 'There was no way I was going to be in a cell with a junkie. Not with a needle around.'

The junkie nodded and pretended to listen as a no-nonsense Field issued his demand. He was once again the

Rugby League captain, firing off a non-negotiable order, his ferocious bark not needing the threat of a bite.

'I told him he had to apply for a new cell in the morning because I could not room with someone on drugs.'

The junkie nodded.

'Sure, man,' he said. 'No worries. I won't do anything near you, man. And I'll get out of your hair soon. You'll get no problems from me, man.'

Field nodded. Then he went to sleep.

The druggie was lying, of course.

'I woke up to the sound of him shitting everywhere. He obviously had his shot when I nodded off, and he couldn't make the toilet.'

Fuck me. Did I really just see that?

Field ignored the smell and went back to sleep.

'I woke up the next morning, and there was shit *every-where*. It was absolutely disgusting.'

The fresh sunlight revealed the full extent of the dev-*ass*-tation.

'He had shit all over himself,' Field says. 'And it was all over the cell too. He hadn't even made an attempt to clean it up. He hadn't even had a go at wiping himself.'

Field was furious.

'I take a lot of pride in the way I keep my cell. I'm a pretty tidy person, and I always make sure I keep my room neat and clean. I try to be well organised, and there I was waking up with shit all over the place. It was all over my stuff.'

The junkie inmate put in a request to leave the cell as soon as he woke up. Field was left to clean up the shit.

'What I find difficult is all the drugs that are around,' Field says. 'That's what creates most of the problems. Obviously I stay right out of it, and it isn't a problem for me, but there are always blokes getting bashed and stabbed over drug debts.

'And everything gets in here, all types of drugs. I've been offered them plenty of times – it happened as soon as I got in – but everyone in here knows how I feel, so they keep it away from me now.

'One of the disgusting things that's happening at the moment involves a drug called "bupa" [buprenorphine],' Field continues. 'It's a morphine-type thing. A lot of blokes who don't need it will get it. They'll take it and hold it under their tongue instead of swallowing it. They'll then go and give it to the junkies in exchange for a head-job. I think they dissolve it and inject it and get a similar high to heroin.'

Field cleaned up the shit and moved on.

'I have a very good arrangement at the moment. I share a room with a bikie and we get on great. Things are working out well. We have a bed on either side of the cell, a little walkway in the middle and some cupboards, drawers, things like that. We have a TV, which is good. We are both into our footy and the same kind of stuff, so that really gets us through. We can't wait for footy season to start because that really gives you something to look forward to; it makes it a lot easier to do your time. He's clean like me and we just get on. I have no hesitation calling him a friend. Life in jail is a lot easier when you're sharing your cell with a mate.'

Still, life in prison can be shitty . . .

'Yeah, there's only one toilet in the cell. There's no privacy, but we have made do by erecting a sheet as a bit of a screen. You don't want to be watching another bloke taking a dump.'

Standovers and Sexual Assaults

Craig looks at the clock.

'Only about 15 minutes left, mate,' he says, the one-hour visit almost at its end. 'What else do you want to know?'

Where do I start?

'What's the worst thing you've seen in prison?' I ask.

Yeah, good question.

Fieldsy finally rips open the big bag of Maltesers. He crunches while he thinks.

'The worst thing I've seen in prison didn't take place here,' he says, referring to Cessnock. 'Nah. I reckon the worst thing I ever saw in prison was at Silverwater. I did a bit of time there, waiting to get my classo [classification], and I saw a bloke get stabbed in the throat.'

Field explains the Silverwater set-up – pods with see-through perspex doors – before unleashing a tale of grizzle and gore.

'Silverwater is a pretty crazy place. You get all sorts in there, and I was expecting to see some things – but I wasn't expecting anything like this. There were sweepers serving food to the pods, one on each side of the corridor. One of them had just shoved my food in, and I was about to rip in.' He grabs another Malteser. 'But I heard all this noise, so I left the food and looked out of my cell.

139

'The sweepers had seen each other and dropped their trays – that was the noise I'd heard. I watched as they ran at each other, throwing punches at first, but then one of them pulled out a shiv. He jammed it straight into the others guy's neck. There was blood everywhere and the bloke dropped. I thought he was going to die.'

I look at Craig and say, 'Shit. That's fucked up.'

'Yeah,' he replies. 'It was. I've seen a lot of violence in my life . . . both on the street and on the footy field. I played a tough game and saw plenty of things in Rugby League. You think you're probably prepared to see violent things like this, but I wasn't prepared at all.

'It was really heavy and it shocked me. It was then that I knew how serious jail could be, and that I needed to be careful. On a football field people may want to hurt you, but in here they want to *kill* you. If you do the wrong thing or upset someone, well, they won't just be coming to fight . . . They'll be coming to kill.'

I can't imagine this bloke in front of me, who's vowed not to punch a person again, ever stabbing someone in the neck with a shiv. *Does he really belong here? For a single punch? Not a king hit or a coward shot. A pub-fight punch . . .*

'I don't think I should be here.' Field shrugs. 'But others do and so I am. Maybe a few will change their minds when they hear my story. I'm still fighting, and hopefully I can launch a new appeal. I think there's enough evidence to get me out. But right now I'm here in jail and, honestly, I've been very lucky.

'I first went to Grafton, and that was a real old scary-looking place with a bad reputation. I didn't know what to expect, but when I got there I was fine. Most people were pretty good to me. Sure, there were one or two blokes who wanted to give me a hard time because of who I was, but most were happy to meet me and talk footy. I think the majority respected me, and I never had to prove I was tough or anything like that by fighting.'

Surely someone has had a go? Just to be known as the bloke who got it over that NRL star?

'Nah,' he says. 'I seriously haven't had any problems. I think everyone knew who I was when I came in, but I've just kept my head down and stayed out of things. You don't want to get caught up in anything. I don't get involved in any of the shit that goes on. If anything, I try to help people. I try to do what I can to make their lives better or their time in here easier.'

Tick, tick, tick – time is running out. So much to ask . . .

'Sounds like you're doing okay,' I say. 'But what about him?' I gesture with my eyes towards a skinny white kid with fluff on his face. He's talking about appeals to his parents, about getting the fuck out of there. 'How does a bloke like that survive?'

'He doesn't, mate,' Field says. 'He doesn't survive. That poor bugger is stood over all the time; anything he gets is taken from him. He has to give up all his buy-ups, food . . . whatever he gets. It's sad but if you don't have respect or can't handle yourself, you will get picked on. It's just the way it is.'

I look at the kid and wonder what he did. What was his crime?

'He couldn't punch his way out of a paper bag,' I say. 'Why doesn't he go into protection?'

Field shakes his head furiously. 'You'd rather *die* than go into protection. That's the worst thing you can do. Heaps of guys do it.'

So why not the kid with bum-fluff on his face?

'Yeah, he probably should've earned some respect for not going into protection.' Field shrugs. 'He has earned it from me. If anyone actually needed protection, I guess it would be someone like him. But he would rather be stood over than forever have to be known as a Dog. He'll eventually get that respect, and the pain he cops now will be nothing compared to what he would cop for the rest of his life if he put his hand up for protection.'

I have a newfound respect for bum-fluff boy.

'Do people rape him?' I ask.

Field looks down at the table; all the food is gone.

'Sexual assault?' he asks. 'I haven't seen it, but you know it goes on. A lot of people in here are gay, and they go out of their way looking for it. They're more than happy to be involved in it and offer themselves up to guys. A lot of others, mostly blokes who are in for life, do things that they wouldn't do if they weren't stuck in a place like this. But that bloke? I don't know. You'd have to ask him.'

'Time's up!' a guard yells. He points at the gigantic steel door. The void . . .

'That's it, mate,' Field says. 'I tell ya what – ring my missus and give her your number. I'll put you on my phone list and give you a call.'

A guard stands over the table and we shake hands.

'Got to go,' he says. 'Pleasure to meet you.' He thanks me again for the snakes and socks.

Phone Calls and Field's Future

Ring! Ring!

I answer my mobile phone.

'You are about to receive a call from an inmate at Cessnock Correctional Centre,' a pre-recorded woman with an American accent fires. 'If you don't want to take this call, hang up now . . . *beep* . . . Go ahead, please.'

A Yank? Seriously?

'Phelpsy?' Field asks over the top of another *beep*.

'Yeah, mate,' I reply. 'How you going?'

I'd called Craig's wife two days after my visit. I'd told her who I was and that I had visited Craig. She told me he'd got the socks and thanked me for the gift. I spoke to her for 20 minutes, and Craig was right: she was doing it tougher than him, all alone, looking after four of his five kids. I gave her my phone number and email address.

'Contact me whenever you like,' I'd said. 'Let me know if there's anything I can do.'

I knew there wasn't much I could do . . . but I offered anyway. The only person who can help Field is a Queen's Counsel he can't afford.

'Okay,' she'd said. 'Thanks. I'll tell Craig to call you on Friday at 3pm. Maybe have your phone handy most of the afternoon, because they can't just pick up the phone. He has to wait, and sometimes he'll ring earlier than he says, other times later.'

I then called a Cessnock corrections officer following my conversation with Ellen. I needed to make sure Craig hadn't been feeding me shit.

'No, mate,' the officer said. 'He's a very good inmate. He causes no trouble at all; we haven't had a problem with him. A few of the guards love chatting to him. They talk a lot of footy and stuff like that. They enjoy his company. What he has told you, about prison anyway, sounds spot-on. No one has any complaints about Craig.'

However, they do watch him closely . . .

'Yeah, when he's out in the yard playing footy!' The guard laughed. 'The old boy still has it. He gets out there, bossing them all around, before putting them through gaps and over for tries. He doesn't run as much as he used to, but he's still a sight to watch. It's not every day we get an NRL halfback in here.'

'Yeah, I'm good mate,' Field continues over the surprisingly clear line. But that's to be expected because every phone call is recorded. *You don't want a crackle in the line ruining a confession.*

'No complaints.' I tell him I have spoken to a guard.

'Which one?' he asks.

'I can't tell you that. But I can tell you that he confirmed a lot of what you said.'

'Okay,' Craig says. 'I understand. Most of them are pretty good to me, hey? A few in particular always come over for a chat. They tell me what's going on outside, and we have a yarn about footy, and they always ask me how I'm being treated and whether or not I need anything. Some others, and there aren't many, are on a power trip. They just want to make your life difficult for the sake of it. They're always the young blokes without stripes. I've had some interesting experiences with paperwork and requests for things.'

We chitchat about footy, his mates, the weather.

Beep.

'They're going to cut it off soon, mate,' he says.

'Really? It's only been six minutes.'

'Yeah, it's not a lot of time. I'll ring you back in 15.'

Beep . . . Beep.

Field is gone.

I wait by the phone. Fifteen minutes come and go. Thirty minutes now. Forty-five.

Ring. Ring. The pre-recorded American girl again: 'You are about to receive a call. If you don't want to take this call, hang up now . . . *beep.*'

'Phelpsy,' Fields says as the phone beeps again. 'I think you're trying not to be rude, but this call will be over very quickly, and I don't know when I'll be able to call again. If you need to know anything else, mate, just ask.'

I want to know heaps. But I'll have to settle for what he can tell me in the next six minutes.

First, I ask him about footy.

'I would love to be involved again,' Field says. 'A lot of blokes are still getting in trouble – and they shouldn't be. There are simple solutions to a lot of these things, and I know I can help a lot of players. This is something that really means a lot to me. I could speak to them from the heart and give them the advice and help they need. I look at what happened to Mitchell Pearce [Sydney Roosters player who was stood down for wetting himself on video and simulating sex with a dog] and shake my head. I know I could have helped prevent something like that.

'I still love my footy and always will. I was doing real well when this thing happened, coaching and helping out kids. It's what I enjoy. Two of the kids I've coached have signed with NRL clubs now, which makes me really proud. I would love to get involved again one day, and I think I'll have a lot to offer. I'm pretty sure I'll have some pretty good stories about the consequences of trouble and how to avoid it.'

I look at the call timer on my phone. *Tick. Tick.* I ask him if he's reformed.

'Jail isn't a place where you reform,' Field replies, 'but I don't consider myself a criminal, and I'll never become one. But I certainly know far more about it than I did before. You're always hearing blokes talking about the crimes they've committed and how they've been done. They all exchange tips. They also meet a lot of contacts of people they'll commit crimes with in the future. It's sad, but the authorities don't care. They just want us all locked up until we're allowed out. They don't care if you leave a better person – not many do. But, mate, I have my trade, my footy and my family. I won't be coming back.'

Tick. Tick.

'Mate, they tell me you're a bit of a leader round the joint,' I say. 'The officer told me you help a lot of blokes around at work. What's the job you have?'

'I work in the print shop from Mondays to Fridays, six hours a day. I'm what they call a "leading hand". I run the

146

inmates in there. I look after them and give them their lunches, their forms – that sort of stuff. It's bit of responsibility but something I really enjoy. I had a leadership role in footy, and it feels like I'm using those skills again. I also get on with all the inmates, which helps. It makes things easier.'

Tick. Tick.

'Print shop,' I say.

'Yeah, mate. We print everything, both inside jobs and outside jobs. We print programs, posters, and business cards for all the corrections officers around the state. We do booklets, magazines . . . everything'.

Beep. Beep.

'What's the pay like?' I fire.

'I get paid about 60 bucks a week. And that's more than most because of the leadership role.'

Sixty dollars a week? Is he serious?

The man who used to earn more than $600,000 a year to throw a ball around is now locked up in prison earning $60 a week to print business cards for prison cops. He's gone from being a man with an estimated wealth of $4 million to an inmate who needs to save to buy deodorant and non-standard-issue shampoo.

Beep.

The line is dead. Craig is gone. I shake my head before putting down my mobile phone.

I'm hoping I'll speak to him again when he's out. Maybe the next time I ring him I'll be speaking as an NRL reporter to a – who knows? – NRL coach. And we'll talk footy rather than prisons.

7

HOLY TERROR
Goulburn

ISIS, Islam and Isolation

Slowly, carefully and, most importantly, *quietly*, he rubbed the plastic against the wall. Outnumbered, outmuscled and facing death, he stealthy sharpened his shiv in the dead of night.

Wruup!

He dragged the hard plastic against the concrete wall.

Wruuup!

Harder this time.

Wruuuup!

Harder again . . .

The sand-smashed, high-aggregate render turned the toilet brush into a lethal, skin-slashing weapon. He was now ready to kill. Designed to polish the porcelain, the foot-long scrubber was his only chance at surviving an attack from the most terrifying prison gang in the world: an all-Australian ISIS.

According to inmates and prison officers alike, the terror outfit ISIS has become a jail gang with the power to rival outfits like the Assyrian criminal syndicate Dlasthr (The Last Hour) and several bikie gangs. A terror plot that involved the kidnapping and beheading of a prison guard was recently uncovered, and the growing group is also threatening to murder 'jail infidels' who do not join their radical Islamic faction. There are at least 30 members of the ISIS gang in Goulburn Jail alone, and all non-Muslims have been removed from the Lebanese Yard after a religiously motivated gang war broke out in 2015.

Two 'Christian' members of the Dlasthr – an offshoot of the Assyrian Kings – stabbed one of Sydney's most infamous murderers in Goulburn Jail in September 2015, allegedly because they were told they would be beheaded for not converting to Islam.

Welcome to the world's most terrifying prison yard . . .

WHACK! The toilet-brush-turned-weapon ripped through flesh. Adnan 'Eddie' Darwiche – the infamous double killer who had waged a murderous war against the Razzak family over drugs and drive-bys – did not see it coming.

Bang!

Next he was stabbed with a shiv that used to be a Breville sandwich toaster handle.

Whack! Bang! Whack! Bang! Whack! Bang!

Eight strikes in total.

Darwiche was a victim of extreme violence in a new type of prison gang warfare.

'It was all terror-related,' said a Goulburn officer. 'The word on the street was that Darwiche had been radicalised, like most in that yard, and they were going to take a hostage – one of the six Christians in the yard – and behead him. They were going to use mobile phones to post it on the internet. They were going to get them because they'd refused to convert to Islam and join ISIS.'

But the infidels struck first in a broad daylight ambush outside the visits centre, in front of four prison guards.

'[Darwiche] was walking back from a visit and two blokes from his yard jumped him,' the officer said. 'At the rear of the yard, they started stabbing him in the neck and the shoulder. The intel said it was to do with the Muslims versus Christians war that is going on. The Muslims were going to kill one of the Christians and film it on their phone. There was also intel branching off from that, saying they were going to get an officer. There was an intercepted Arabic message saying they were going to abduct an officer and behead him.'

These bearded men, the Koran they clutch the only thing longer than their records, are the new breed of prison 'gang-bangers'.

'Darwiche has taken his street gang and joined ISIS,' the guard said. 'They are made up of all different gangs, like Brothers 4 Life and Will To Kill. They come through and start associating with radical Islam. They have never come out and officially *claimed* they are an ISIS gang – neither have our bosses – but that's what's happening. We have found ISIS flags, tattoos and lots of other indicators.'

Powerful prison gangs with Islamic beliefs are beginning to merge because of shared ideologies. Self-styled sheikhs like Wassim Fayad, who was jailed for a shocking 'sharia law' crime that saw him whip a man 40 times with an electrical cord for drinking alcohol and taking drugs, are leading the religious call to arms.

'ISIS is massive in Goulburn,' said another guard, who did not want to be named for fear of losing his job. 'The Lebanese never fought with each other, but now they'll go after each other because of religion. The Christians are out to get the Muslims, and the Muslims are out to get the Christians. I had never witnessed Lebanese guys fighting Lebanese guys until last year when it all began to kick off.'

Prison officers conducted a series of cell searches in 2015, and they uncovered disturbing material that had terror undertones.

'We were doing ramps on cells every week and finding all sorts of shit,' the officer continued. 'We found ISIS flags painted on walls and SD cards in mobile phones with terror-related footage. A lot of the guys were also getting the ISIS flag tattooed on their bodies. We've confiscated a lot of material deemed to be inappropriate – it's something we've come down very heavy on.

'We can't stop them from recruiting others to their cause.

SUNDAY SEPTEMBER 13 2015 $2.80

The Sunday Telegraph

Picture: Gary Ramage

MARTIN BRYANT
FIRST PHOTO IN 18 YEARS

Australia's worst killer back in max security

'Creeping' predator attacks prison nurses

Dubbed Porky Pig, balloons to 160kg

STILL EVIL

THE gunman responsible for killing 35 people in the Port Arthur massacre continues to create terror inside jail, it can be revealed. Martin Bryant, whose weight has ballooned to as much as 160kg, has been moved to maximum security after a series of savage assaults. Despite his massive size, one prison nurse was attacked after Bryant crept up on him from behind, the carpet concealing his approach. Prison sources say Bryant lives a lonely and pathetic existence, often drugged to the point of "being a vegetable", preying on weaker inmates and swapping family-sized blocks of chocolate for performing sexual favours. SARAH BLAKE'S SPECIAL INVESTIGATION AND MORE PHOTOS PAGES 2-5

ENTERTAIN YOUR KIDS SCHOOL HOLIDAY FUN GUIDE

The front page of the *Sunday Telegraph* on 13 September 2015 revealed a shocking portrait of Martin Bryant, the man responsible for the 1996 Port Arthur Massacre, which claimed 35 lives and injured 23 others. Now almost 50, Bryant is a fat, bald deviant dubbed 'Porky Pig', who trades sexual favours for chocolate. (NEWS LTD/NEWSPIX)

Exterior view of Risdon Prison in Hobart, Tasmania, where Martin Bryant is serving 35 life sentences plus 1035 years without parole. (GARY RAMAGE/NEWSPIX)

An aerial shot of Goulburn Correctional Centre's Supermax complex, where some of Australia's most evil men – serial killers, rapists, mass murderers, drug kingpins and terrorists – are locked away. (BARRY CHAPMAN/FAIRFAX PHOTOS)

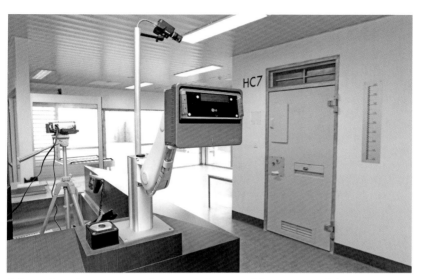

A fingerprint and eye scanner inside Cessnock Correctional Centre, a state-of-the-art maximum-security prison in Cessnock, New South Wales. These 'biometric security' measures record the identity of anyone who enters the facility. (STEPHEN COOPER/NEWSPIX)

One of the accommodation blocks inside Cessnock. (STEPHEN COOPER/NEWSPIX)

Inside the walls of HM Prison Pentridge. Built in 1850 in the Melbourne suburb of Coburg, it housed inmates – as well as Ned Kelly's buried remains – until it was decommissioned in 1997.

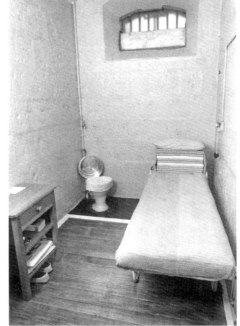

A maximum-security cell inside 'H Division', the infamous punishment section of Pentridge responsible for inflicting many physical and psychological scars on inmates. To walk through its gates would be to experience a 'reception biff' by the welcoming guards – all bats, blood and bruises.

Pentridge escapee Ronald Ryan, on his way back to Melbourne to stand trial for the murder of prison officer George Hodson. Ryan was the last person in Australia to be legally executed by hanging on 3 February 1967.
(NEWS LTD/NEWSPIX)

A prison officer stands in Ronald Ryan's former cell in H Division. Notorious inmate John Killick, who viciously attacked a prison officer with an iron bar, spent 48 terrifying hours in Ryan's cell, convinced he was also condemned to hang.
(DAVID GERAGHTY/NEWSPIX)

Aerial view of Silverwater Metropolitan Remand Centre in Sydney, where Lucy Dudko forced helicopter pilot Tim Joyce at gunpoint to assist in breaking out her lover, the armed robber John Killick. (TROY BENDEICH/NEWSPIX)

Tim Joyce, pilot of the hijacked helicopter used to free John Killick. (CHRIS PAVLICH/NEWSPIX)

Lucy Dudko is taken from the NSW District Court in Sydney after being found guilty of the helicopter hijacking. After serving her time as a 'model inmate' at the Dillwynia Correctional Centre in Western Sydney, she turned to God and away from John. (CRAIG GREENHILL/NEWSPIX)

Former bank robber John Killick at Brisbane Airport in January 2015, following his release from Woodford Correctional Centre. (LIAM KIDSTON/NEWSPIX)

Rodney 'Goldie' Atkinson . . . an alleged hitman and an undisputed hardman, feared by both prisoners and guards alike, pictured here in Nomads bikie gang attire.

A promotional poster for an MMA fight featuring a lean, mean, post-Goulburn Goldie. The fight was ultimately cancelled by police, who thought the event would present a risk to the public. The authorities also refused to issue him with a fighter's licence.

A fighting-fit Goldie, preparing for life on the outside, where he's contemplating opening a gym or operating a protein supplement shop. (PHOTOS COURTESY RODNEY ATKINSON)

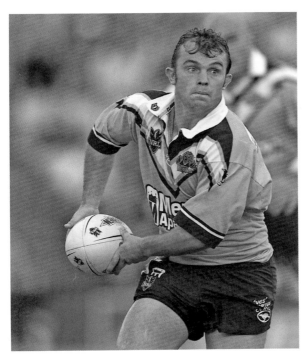

Craig Field lines up a pass during a Wests Tigers v. Newcastle NRL game in 2000. (GREGG PORTEOUS/ NEWSPIX)

Field was enjoying his post-NRL career as an electrician and coach for the Cudgen Hornets in northern New South Wales when, in 2014, he delivered a fatal punch to local cattle farmer Kelvin Kane during a Kingscliff pub brawl. He was found guilty of manslaughter and sentenced to ten years in Cessnock Correctional Centre. (JEFF DARMANIN/NEWSPIX)

Top: David Hooker (left) was pulled aside early on in Minda by his friends from the streets and taught the 'prison code' – the unwritten laws that would save his life. 'Stick with us and you'll be sweet. Keep to yourself when you aren't with us, and don't fuck with anyone we've pointed out. And if anything goes wrong, we'll sort it out.'

Middle: Hooker (back row, fourth from right) with his crew.

Bottom: Hooker ultimately survived his incarceration. Now in his mid-30s, he has a young family, runs a legitimate business and lives well away from his old stomping grounds. (PHOTOS COURTESY DAVID HOOKER)

Male & Female CSNSW GENERIC WEEKLY GROCERY BUY-UP LIST

Name: _____

Wing/Unit/Pod: _____ Date: _____

Location: _____

MIN Signature: _____

EXAMPLE:

MIN
1 0 0 2 0 1

INSTRUCTIONS
- Use a Blue or Black pen OR 3B pencil ONLY!!!
- Write numbers in boxes provided, then mark oval corresponding to the number in each column
- Do not use red pen or felt tip pen
- Fill the ovals completely

MARK LIKE THIS ONLY:
- Do not fold or bend
- Make no stray marks

GBA	QTY	TOBACCO REPLACEMENT	UNIT
00619		Nicorette Coldrops 4mg	20pk

GBR	QTY	TOILETRIES & HYGIENE	UNIT
00531		In-House Conditioner - White Velvet	250ml
00532		In-House Shampoo - White Velvet	250ml
00533		In-House Shampoo - Anti Dandruff	250ml
00534		In-House Body Wash - Orange & Mandarin	250ml
00535		In-House Laundry Liquid - Fusion	250ml
00536		In-House Fabric Softener - Lavender	250ml
00031		Baby Powder	400g
00033		Conditioner - Pantene	200ml
00035		Conditioner - Herbal Essences	300ml
00036		Conditioner - Sunsilk	200ml
00411		Conditioner - Dove	320ml
00037		Cotton Tips - Swisspers	50's
00620		Deodorant - Brut 33 Stick	75g
00040		Deodorant - Speed Stick 24 7 Menscent	55g
00042		Deodorant - Lady Stick	45g
00045		Moisturiser - Vaseline Aloe Smooth	225ml
00621		Moisturiser - Vaseline Cocoa Body Lotion	225ml
00047		Nail Clipper - Toe	each
00048		Razor - Disposable	5pk
00420		Razor - Mach 3	each
00421		Razor Blades Only - Mach 3	4pk
00050		Shampoo - 2 in 1 Turning Point	400ml
00051		Shampoo - Anti Dandruff Neutrogena	200ml
00053		Shampoo - Pantene	200ml
00055		Shampoo - Herbal Essences	300ml
00056		Shampoo - Sunsilk	200ml
00224		Shampoo - Dove	320ml
00058		Shaving Cream - Tube	65g
00059		Soap - Medicated Sapoderm	3pk
00060		Soap - Cashmere	2pk
00343		Soap - Palmolive Gold	4pk
00425		Soap - Dove	
00537		Hand & Body Wash - Goats Milk Sensitive Skin	500ml
		Shower Gel - Palmolive	500ml
00622		Shower Gel - Lynx Africa	400ml
00065		Toothpaste - Whitening Colgate	110g
00066		Toothpaste - Sensodyne	100g
00067		Toothpaste - Extreme Clean Maclean	160g
00068		Toothpaste - Colgate Regular	120g
00429		Dental Floss	each
00538		Mouth Wash - Alcohol Free	500ml
00432		Lip Balm	each
00436		Sorbolene Cream	100g

GBE	QTY	HEALTHIER OPTIONS	UNIT
00539		In-House Sugar Free Fruit Drops	100g
00325		In-House Eclipse Spearmint - Sugar Free	19g
00540		In-House Pumpkin Seeds	130g
00541		In-House Sunflower Seeds	225g
00542		In-House Walnut	100g
00543		In-House Roasted Peanut in Shell	250g
00544		In-House Caribbean Brunch Mix	200g
00623		In-House Kellogg's All Bran	300g
00284		In-House Mixed Rice Crackers	250g
00624		In-House Sugarless Stevia Organic Sweetener	25x2g
00625		Coke Zero - Can	375ml
00384		Pepsi Max - Can	375ml
00127		Tea Bag - Green	25pk
00128		Tea Bag - Camomile	10pk
00129		Tea Bag - Black	50pk
00668		Tea Bag - Jasmine Green	25pk
		Instant Drink Powder - Orange	15g

GBE	QTY	HEALTHIER OPTIONS	UNIT
00369		Instant Drink Powder - Lime Lemon	15g
00161		Baked Beans in Tomato Sauce - Heinz - Tin	220g
00162		Baked Beans in Tomato Sauce - SPC - Tin	140g
00626		Giant Baked Beans - Paliria - Tin	280g
00240		Spaghetti in Tom Sauce & Cheese - Tin	220g
00175		Champignon - Tin	285g
00179		Capsicum Diced - Tin	125g
00181		Corn Creamed - Tin	125g
00385		Corn Kernels - Tin	125g
00627		Tomatoes Whole Peeled - Tin	400g
00628		Sliced Beetroot - Tin	225g
00461		Mixed Vegetables - Tin	420g
00462		Red Kidney Beans - Tin	300g
00629		Chick Peas - Tin	300g
00630		Brown Lentils - Tin	400g
00197		Four Bean Mix - Tin	300g
00353		Milk - Long Life Skim	1ltr
00199		Milk Powder - Skim	300g
00631		Milk - Soy	1ltr
00389		V8 Vegetable Juice Original 250ml	3pk
00632		Uncle Toby Quick Oats - Original	10pk
00521		Uncle Toby Quick Oats - Berry Variety	12pk
		Weet Bix	575g
00551		Muesli Apricot	650g
00552		Up & Go Strawberry	250ml
00243		Up & Go Chocolate	250ml
00496		Spread - Hazelnut	220g
00224		Salmon - Pink - Tin	210g
00262		Salmon - Smoked - Tin	125g
00261		Tuna - Capsicum Chilli - Tin	95g
00497		Tuna - Onion Tomato Sauce - Tin	95g
00498		Tuna - Lemon - Pouch	100g
00499		Tuna - Tomato - Pouch	100g
00500		Tuna - Olive Oil - Pouch	100g
00356		Tuna - Sweet Chilli - Pouch	100g
00229		Tuna in Spring Water - Tin	185g
00633		Tuna in Chilli - Tin	185g
00634		Sardines in Tomato Sauce - Tin	125g
00640		Mexican Tuna Meal (With Brown Rice)	110g
00635		Italian Tuna Meal (With Pasta)	110g
		Rice Cake - Salt & Vinegar	120g
00636		Rice Cake	195g
00637		Biscuit - Rice Crackers Chicken	100g
00276		Biscuit - Rice Crackers BBQ	100g
00281		Biscuit - Salada	250g
00638		Biscuit - Vita Wheat Original	250g
00639		Biscuit - Shapes Light & Crispy 5 Ch & 5 Crm	120g
00202		Brown Rice Chips - Parmesan & Sundried Tomato	156g
00464		Brown Rice Chips - Sea Salt	156g
00641		Popcorn - Original	10pk
00527		Sesame Seeds Bar	45g
00642		Sesame Crisp	40g
00643		Nut Bar - Almond Apricot	50g
00546		Nut Bar - Nut Delight Gluten Free	40g
00547		Nut Bar - Macadamia Dream	50g
00548		Hi Protein Bar - Choc Berry	50g
00549		Hi Protein Bar - Original Nut Crunch	50g
00550		Lo Carb Bar - Caramel	30g
		Lo Carb Bar - Raspberry Choc	30g
		Bounce Bar - Coconut & Macadamia	40g
		Lo Carb Bar - Cranberry & Greek Yoghurt	40g

GBE	QTY	CULTURALLY FRIENDLY	UNIT
00555		In-House Dates Pitted	250g
00556		In-House Garlic Granules	100g
00644		In-House Mixed Herbs	50g
00561		In-House Zaiter (Thyme)	200g
00553		Turkish Delight with Almond	each
00557		Olives - Black	350g
00178		Olives - Green	250g
00357		Chinese Mixed Vegetables - Tin	250g
00359		Bamboo Shoots - Tin	425g
00554		Halal Meat - Chicken Luncheon - Tin	230g
00494		Halal Meat - Corned Beef - Tin	200g
00203		Cous Cous	340g
00376		Tortilla Wrap	500g
00377		Rice Vermicelli	6pk
00645		Noodles - 2 minute Beef	250g
00646		Noodles - 2 minute Chicken	5pk
00209		Noodles - Bowl Spicy Beef	5pk
00210		Noodles - Bowl Stewed Pork	120g
00398		Noodles - Hot & Spicy	120g
		Noodles - Singapore	85g
		Noodles - Wokka Hokkien	85g

The buy-up sheet. From Herbal Essences conditioner and mouth wash (alcohol-free) to tinned beetroot and halal meat, this is the list of items an inmate is allowed to purchase.

Mobile phones, smuggled from the outside, are a major problem in prison, with inmates running drug rings and contracting hits on rivals from the comfort of their cell. Here, a guard illustrates how a phone can be hidden inside a sardine can. (JEFF HERBERT/NEWSPIX)

Drugs removed from an inmate's rectum. (PHOTO SUPPLIED BY ROY FOXWELL)

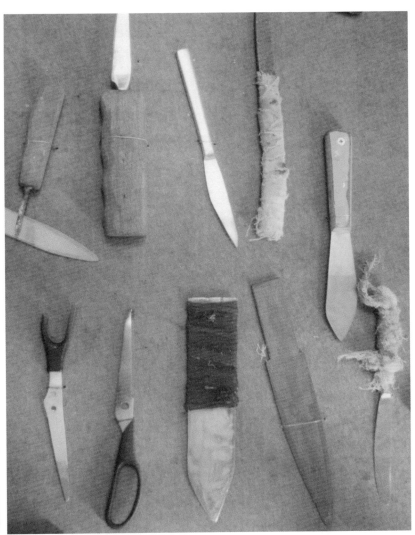

A collection of prison shivs seized by Long Bay guards during a raid. (PHOTO SUPPLIED BY DAVE FARRELL)

Brothers 4 Life gang founder Bassam Hamzy has been described as the most dangerous inmate in the correctional system.

Mohamed Elomar, one of the 'Terror Five' militants arrested in 2005. In a letter signed by all 13 AA-class inmates locked up in Goulburn's Supermax for terror-related crimes and detailing a long list of grievances, Elomar was singled out for his failure to be reintegrated into general population despite his good behaviour.

Mass murderer Martin Bryant kicks a football in the exercise yard in the Mersey Unit – a 'special needs' section of Risdon Prison. (GARY RAMAGE/NEWSPIX)

Tony Halloun is escorted from Queen Square Supreme Court in Sydney after he was found guilty of murdering Shahnaz Qidwai during a home invasion of her waterfront mansion in 2012. Halloun arrived at Goulburn a marked man and was dealt a hefty serving of prison justice in the form of an epic beat-down by feared inmate Goldie Atkinson. According to Goldie: 'He had to pay.' (BRAD HUNTER/ NEWSPIX)

Hey Dad! actor Robert Hughes arrives at the Downing Centre Local Court in Sydney to give evidence in his trial over child sex offences. Hughes was ultimately found guilty and sentenced to a minimum of six years' jail for molesting four girls between 1984 and 1990. The '*Hey Dad!* Wall' was built at Goulburn Jail to stop enraged inmates from hurling faeces, urine and boiling water at the paedophile. (ROSS SCHULTZ/NEWSPIX)

Disgraced HIH insurance founder Ray Williams after his release from Silverwater. Williams served just under three years for his role in Australia's largest corporate collapse. As Ray found out, not even white-collar criminals can avoid punch-ups when revenge is on the cards. (SAM MOOY/NEWSPIX)

Status update . . . Beau Wiles posted this photo of himself on Facebook – clad only in a hat and red undies – from a smuggled phone. The message to his girlfriend, Rebecca Watts, read, 'Love u my my [sic] princess.' The two pulled off a brief 30-hour escape from the minimum-security section at Goulburn before Wiles was caught and sentenced to an additional six months.

The extreme guys just start talking to normal Muslims and put ideas into their heads. They carry on about injustices, give them a sense of belonging and try and tell them to go to Syria and fight for ISIS when they're out.'

Sometimes they even get bashed if they don't listen . . .

'There have been instances of blokes being belted because they aren't willing to take up the cause. [ISIS] prey on the young ones, and there are consequences if they don't listen.'

Prison officials went on the warpath when I first revealed Goulburn's links to ISIS in a story published in the *Sunday Telegraph* in October 2015. In a statement – not an official media release – called 'For the Record: "Goulburn Jail becomes an offshoot of ISIS" by James Phelps', the Department of Corrective Services Assistant Commissioner Kevin Corcoran claimed a number of factual errors in my article.

Here's what was said:

1. The organisation ISIS has not infiltrated the state's prisons and is not a gang.
2. There is no known member of the organisation ISIS in a New South Wales prison.
3. There has been no credible threat to murder staff or inmates in a New South Wales prison because they are non-Muslims.
4. There has been no threat to behead staff or inmates.
5. Criminal gangs are sometimes formed based on religious background, but there have been no religiously motivated gang wars at Goulburn Jail.

Really? Just a day before the statement was released, a Corrective Services media man replied to a number of questions put to him by the *Sunday Telegraph*.

Here is the complete response:

> Corrective Services NSW devotes considerable effort to keeping inmates safe. This includes intelligence gathering and the separation of inmates known to pose a threat from those who are at risk.
>
> It is correct that Adnan Darwiche was attacked in Goulburn Correctional Centre and that gas was used to subdue some inmates in the aftermath of the attack.
>
> There is no evidence that a beheading threat was made at Goulburn Correctional Centre. Initial intelligence to that effect was received, but on investigation it proved to be wrong.
>
> A small number of inmates share the views of ISIS, but there is no evidence they are formally linked to that organisation.
>
> CSNSW cannot comment on any of the other matters raised for security reasons.

So before the article was published there were 'a small number of inmates who share the view of ISIS', but afterwards there was 'no known member of ISIS in a NSW jail'.

'They don't carry ID cards around,' said a prison officer after being told of the department's response. 'They are certainly clamming to be ISIS, so I'm not sure what's required to officially be classified as a member.'

Yep . . . semantics.

And there was never a threat to behead an officer in the jail? But there was 'initial intelligence to that effect'.

'Do you think the people who made the threat would admit it once confronted?'

Again . . . semantics.

And why was it never denied that all Christian inmates were removed from the Lebanese Yard?

Because they were.

And wouldn't that suggest that there was 'a religiously motivated' problem at Goulburn?

Again . . . semantics.

The department also cast doubt on the allegations in the article because the quotes were anonymous.

Despite its strong denials, Corrective Services NSW was forced to admit they had a problem with ISIS in April when a former Australian soldier was attacked by a man he was sharing a cell with at the Mid North Coast Correctional Centre in Kempsey – a man who claimed to be an ISIS supporter. In a sickening attack that led to a senior prison official being stood down, the radical was charged after carving 'E4E' – a known ISIS slogan meaning 'eye for an eye' – into the forehead of the former digger, who was rushed to hospital following the attack.

Bourhan Hraichie, 18, had been previously caught sending images of beheadings, via the internal mail at Goulburn Jail, to other known ISIS supporters. It is understood the inmate also had a hand-drawn ISIS flag inside his cell.

Hraichie was charged with causing grievous body harm with intent and intentionally choking a person.

Peter Severin confirmed the attack and admitted it 'appears to have had a strong fundamentalist element to it'. The commissioner also added, 'This was a serious mistake and is under investigation.'

In a separate incident during the same week as the attack on the former soldier, inmates were relocated from Kempsey to Kariong Correctional Centre for threatening to stab inmates who would not convert to Islam.

'I don't believe they are taking the issue of extremism seriously,' said Public Service Association Corrections Branch chairman Steve McMahon. 'They have denied for close to 12 months that there is an issue around extremism in New South Wales prisons.'

'There are a lot of people who are radical,' said one former Muslim inmate, who did not want to be identified. 'That's not bullshit at all. They all speak about [committing acts of terror], but I don't think any of them will go through with it.

'The ISIS stuff is true too. [Inmates] claim they are with them and get the flags, the tattoos, but I think it's just attention-seeking more than anything. If they were really followers then they wouldn't be getting in trouble and put in jail to start with. They do recruit. A lot of them try and convert others to Islam. Not all Muslims are strict, and that can create problems with the ones who are. You see, there isn't much to do in prison. Some try and better themselves and other people try to create shit. They use Islam for both.'

This former inmate said he'd overheard conversations concerning terrorism.

'I was in jail for quite a while, and I did meet quite a few radicals, but I never really heard them preach anything about blowing up [places] in Australia. What I did hear them say was that they would go overseas to do it. They would go fight for a cause overseas, because it wasn't right that women and children were dying and no one was doing anything about it. It was all about one super country [America] telling the rest of the world what they can and can't practise.'

He also claimed the officers showed prejudice towards Islamic inmates.

'A lot of people didn't like that I was a Muslim. They would just say, "You're a wannabe Lebo follower," and shit like that. It just comes down to faith. I still practise and I still pray. A lot of the guards were against it. There are a lot of redneck guards in jail, and they don't know a lot about Islam. They go heavy on anyone who is Muslim.'

Extreme Measures for Extremists

Despite not 'officially' having a problem with 'radicals' in New South Wales jails, a series of high-level crackdowns, policies and procedures have significantly reduced the threat of terror in prisons across the state.

'It has been very quiet of late,' said a highly trainer officer who works in a prison emergency response unit. 'Departments like ASIO and the anti-terrorism squad [the Terrorism Intelligence Unit run by the NSW Police Force] are all over them. They are listening to all their calls and not letting them move an inch. They are getting absolutely smashed because so much money is being put into fighting it. Anti-terror squads are turning up to the jails every other day, coming in and interviewing a lot of guys. They are pumping them for information, and in some instances offering them deals.'

It comes as no surprised that anti-terrorism units – both federal and state divisions – have a keen interest in prisons, especially Goulburn. The prison, two hours south-west of Sydney, is home to all of Australia's convicted terrorists. There are at least 13 extreme high-risk inmates at Goulburn who have an AA classification, which is only given to convicted terrorists – and in some instances suspected terrorists yet to be tried.

Some of the radicals are locked up in Supermax – the 'jail-within-a-jail' at Goulburn – including foiled Pendennis terror cell plotters Khaled Cheikho, Moustafa Cheikho, Mohammed Omar Jamal, Mazen Touma and Omar Baladjam.

Another current officer confirmed a series of crackdowns had quelled radicals and terror chatter. 'They've been real quiet since Darwiche got punted from the yards after he was stabbed,' he said. 'They are keeping a very low profile in the Lebanese Yard right now and may have gone back to dealing drugs. They aren't attracting any attention to themselves, and it's understood they are selling ice. There's a fracture in the Islander Yard, and I think the Lebs are filling the void and taking over the drug market.'

A series of extreme measures began to be introduced

from late 2014 after revelations that terrorists were capable of plotting crimes by code from behind bars.

Among the most controversial was the banning of at least one Islamic prayer meeting in a Sydney jail following high-level discussions about blanket bans across the state.

A scheduled 2.30pm prayer meeting at the Dawn de Loas Correctional Centre, a low-security jail near Silverwater, on 19 September 2014 was controversially cancelled by authorities. It came after security staff intercepted a jihadist letter from an Australian-raised inmate with suspected terror links.

Muslim inmates in all jails across New South Wales are allocated a room to conduct organised prayer meetings on Friday afternoons. The meetings were identified as a security risk by police and ASIO because they were unsupervised and often conducted in Arabic. Corrective Services denied the prospect of blanket prayer bans but confirmed the prison system had implemented a controversial 'deradicalisation' program.

'Corrective Services NSW has developed and implemented comprehensive strategies to deal with radicalisation and to strongly focus on deradicalisation of inmates,' a spokesman said. 'Only specially vetted and accredited imams are allowed to lead the prayers. The Corrective Services Intelligence Group evaluates all activities on an ongoing basis and prison management intervenes as required.

'CSNSW has a strict assessment process for when religious leaders seek access to inmates in a correctional centre for religious purposes, under its well-recognised and long-standing chaplaincy program.

'Anyone who applies must undergo strict security checks,

including having their fingerprints taken and a national criminal record enquiry conducted. Any person who has not resided in Australia for a period of five years or more may also be subject to an Interpol check.'

Later, in early 2015, there was an uproar from the Muslim community about bans on extreme high-risk inmates speaking Arabic in prison. Inmates at Goulburn went on a hunger strike after learning that they would be prevented from speaking in, what was for some, their first language.

The strike came after NSW Attorney-General Brad Hazzard revealed a new policy banning the high-risk inmates who had been convicted of terror-related crimes from speaking in any language other than English during visits, phone calls and also in letters. Their families were left fuming.

'This is a concern for some inmates who don't speak much English,' said one family member. 'But a greater concern is that the recitation of the Koran and *duaa* in Arabic could be stopped and made punishable by prison guards.'

Hazzard defended the policy: 'While there is no specific terrorist threat from inside our prisons, these inmates' communications from prison have the potential to have a direct impact on national security and community safety. That is why I want to make sure we know at all times who they are talking to and what is being said.'

Yours Sincerely, from Supermax

The following is a convicted terrorist's extraordinary letter obtained to use in this book. Signed by all 13 AA-class inmates locked in Goulburn's Supermax – also known as the High-Risk Management Unit (HRMU) – the terror inmates complain about the harsh conditions imposed on them by both the New South Wales government, the federal government and by the Department of Corrective Services. It is published here in its entirety as it is the most comprehensive description of what life in Supermax is like for the AA-classified prisoners. Should everything stated in this letter prove to be true . . .

I am writing to complain about the unjust and harsh treatment that I and 12 other inmates are currently suffering at Goulburn's Supermax High-Risk Correctional Centre [March 2015, the Department of Corrective Services changed our security classification to 'Extreme High Risk Restricted' (EHRR), which has resulted in harsher, more oppressive restrictions being placed upon all AA inmates]. I am also writing to protest against the defamatory allegations made against us in the media as a direct result of prison authorities allowing media personnel into our unit only days before we, and indeed the public, were informed about our new classification.

As you may very well be aware, any person charged with terrorism is automatically designated as an AA category EHR inmate. Now the new law is any person charged with terrorism is AA category EHRR, which carries harsher and stricter sanctions and restrictions than the previous, already oppressive, EHR classification.

The prominent issues that most violate our rights and those of our families pertain to:

Visits:

On our previous classification, AA-EHR, any visitors were put through an intense and rigorous screening process including screening through the Commissioner's office and external security agencies including NSW Police, Australian Federal Police and ASIO for security checks.

In the last nine years here, the inmates from Operation Pendennis have only been granted permission for visits for some family members and a couple of non-family visitors through a long and draining process, years of rejections, delays and claims of 'lost paperwork'. There are many applications we are still waiting on – including siblings.

Of those approved, not all were contact visits and many were still 'box visits'. Personally, it took eight years for my brother to get approved from non-contact to contact visitor after eight years of appeals to the Ombudsman. Others are still waiting to this day for family members to be approved.

Visits last for approximately forty-five minutes to one hour. Before the visits we are fully strip searched in the presence of at least three officers, then put in orange overalls, which are locked on at the back of the neck. Upon arrival, our visitors go through three screening points with metal detectors.

All non-contact visits were held in a section with a number of cubicles – inmates on one side and visitors on the other with a perspex window in between.

Contact visits were held in a room where only one inmate and his visitors would occupy at any given time. There are five metal stools and a small metal round table in the middle, all fixed to the ground. The inmate has to sit on the designated white-coloured stool. There are three security cameras fixed on that group in the room. Directly opposite the room is the guard's room, where he is watching the visit both through the clear perspex walls and on the monitors, watching and recording live all that goes on between the inmate and his visitors.

The new EHRR procedure for visits:
The security screening process for visitor's applications is now rescrutinised. All visits are now non-contact, meaning none of our visits are contact, not with our children, parents or wives – no one.

There is a specially designed steel box just for our visits. This box is a small sheetmetal-lined room, walls and ceiling, approximately four metres long and one and a half metres wide. Dividing the room is a steel wall with a perspex window over a wide steel bench so that each side is now less than two-metres deep. On one side of the room is a large one-way mirrored window, and behind that an officer sits with video and audio equipment recording the visit. The inmates must speak through a hand receiver phone and visitors huddle around the intercom to hear us speak. The voices are muffled and difficult to hear on both sides. They are locked in the box without adequate ventilation and cannot go to the toilet if needed or their visit is terminated.

Recently, one inmate was visited by his mother and three sons. After just ten minutes the youngest son, who is eleven years old, started to have an anxiety attack because of the *heat and stuffiness in the confined space. This 'box' cannot fit more than four chairs; most of us have more than six visiting at a time. These conditions make it physically and emotionally unbearable.*

All conversations must now be in English only or the visit is immediately terminated. One of the reasons given for this is that it's part of the Government's strategy to 'de-radicalise' us. Many of the inmates and their families cannot speak English well or even at all and can only speak Arabic or Afghani. In this case, an application can be made to the Commissioner, and only in rare and special cases will he approve a language other than English to be spoken, provided an interpreter is present for immediate translation. Attorney-General Brad Hazzard in the Daily Telegraph *is quoted as saying: 'If an inmate was speaking with his ninety-year-old grandmother who spoke no English . . . We don't want to create a situation where they feel there's no humanity, because there will be.'*

The new language restriction makes visits for the non-English-speaking inmates and their families impossible. For all of us not to be able to say a prayer or supplication or quote verses from the Qur'an while with our visitors is a degrading and despicable act. This is oppression and discrimination.

To have no contact – physically – with our children, parents, families and friends in such conditions is inhumane, intrusive and a deprivation of our rights as human beings. Bear in mind, we have done nothing to deserve this treatment.

Phone calls:

Previously as AA-EHR inmates, any person we wanted to communicate with via the phone had to be applied for and put through the same intense security checks as visitor applications. Along with that are the same rejections, delays and 'lost paperwork'. In most cases, it takes up to six weeks of running around in circles to get a phone contact number approved.

If a phone number is approved, it is set as a present number, unique to the inmate's phone call account.

To make a call from here costs $2.20 and our calls are strictly limited to only six minutes. Depending on what stage an inmate is on in the Behavioural Management Program, the maximum number of calls per week is only seven. Remand inmates only get four calls per week. These are the restrictions on all calls except legal calls.

Our names are placed on a daily list and our turn to make our one call is at the staff's discretion, so arranging a time with our family and friends is impossible and causes huge strain on family relations.

All our personal calls are monitored live by a guard while recording. All calls are forwarded to a Corrective Services wing called CIG – Central Intelligence Group –in Sydney, who would also listen to them and pass anything they deem important over to other authorities.

All of our legal phone calls are also listened to live – where are our 'Legal Privilege' rights?

The new EHRR restriction for phone calls:

As with visits restrictions, phone calls must now be in

English only or the call is immediately terminated. This is denying the inmates and/or their families who have little or no English the right to have telephone contact.

Mail:
Previously, all our non-legal mail was read, photocopied and had to pass approval before being sent or received. It was also sent to CIG in Sydney to be scrutinised. Often mail never reaches our addressees or us, and those that do usually take a minimum of seven to ten days. Others have taken weeks. The same applies with receiving mail. This slow, delayed and sometimes prevented communication causes a lot of anxiety between inmates and their families. Corrective Services claim that legal mail is not read or photocopied, but many times they give it to us already opened, and several times legal mail sent never reached our lawyers.

Now, under the new EHRR restrictions, our mail goes through the same rigorous checks but must now only be written in English. So, along with the prohibition of speaking in another language with family members and friends, it is prohibited to write or receive letters from family and friends in another language. This further depri-vation of communication has severely affected the inmates and their families, causing a lot of distress. Together with the restrictions of speaking only English during visits and phone calls, this has made any reasonable level of commu-nication with family members and friends extremely difficult, if not impossible.

Money:
AA–EHR inmates were allowed to receive from an approved family member or friend the limited amount of $100 per week that was sent electronically to the jail and took the form of electronic currency in our accounts controlled by Corrective Services. The inmates could use this money to buy food items and necessary toiletries and vitamins. This system is called the weekly 'buy-up'.

Every Saturday we are issued with a list of a very limited number of non-perishable food items (mostly junk food) and toiletries. We would tick the items we wanted, then the money is deducted, and we would get it the following Friday. The items are super-inflated in price, earning high-profit margins.

The money in our accounts would also be used to pay for new prison clothes and sneakers, and for phone calls and any photocopying costs. Photocopying costs are from 50c to $1 per page and faxes are $4 for the first page and $1 for every page thereafter. This makes preparations for court very expensive.

Under the new EHRR restrictions, we are no longer allowed to receive ANY money from anyone. We only receive the standard $13 per week from the government to all inmates. Contrary to comments made by the Corrective Services Minister, we are NOT provided with halal meals; we actually have to PAY for them at a cost of $32 per week. This is impossible to afford at $13 per week.

The $13 per week is unable to meet the following costs for basic necessities and makes it near impossible to:

- *Make calls to family and friends; impossible for families living overseas*
- *Make calls to lawyers and prepare for court matters*
- *Purchase the halal meals on the weekly menu ($32/week)*
- *Buy the emergency back-up food to replace inedible (non-halal) food we are provided with by the jail as part of the standard menu*
- *Buy vitamins to make up for some of the much-lacking nutrition and energy from jail meals and to help fight illness*
- *Buy deodorant, soap, shampoo and other necessary toiletries.*

Parole:
In normal circumstances, to be eligible for parole we need to get out of Supermax and into the 'general population' and complete programs to prepare us for release. Six of the inmates here have already been waiting for over nine years to exit here with no justifiable explanation given for holding us here for so long.

The EHRR classification requires us to stay in this complex, which makes our eligibility for parole impossible.

In conclusion, these new EHRR restrictions, added to the already harsh and oppressive regime that we have been subjected to for over nine years, are oppressive and inhumane and have cut us off from our families and friends, prevented us the right to proper legal access and stopped us from buying the most basic of necessities, such as religiously appropriate food and toiletry items.

Remand Inmates:
There are six inmates here on remand. Remand inmates are supposed to be held at a remand jail local to Sydney, in general population, and with access to all the services and means to proper legal representation.

All these inmates are under 25 years old with no criminal history. It is their first time in jail and they are being subjected to harsh and onerous, unjust and oppressive treatment.

To stay mentally sane and strong in here is a daily struggle. Yet these young men are also expected to prepare for court matters, something that is now made impossible with these new restrictions and without adequate communication with family for support, which is greatly needed.

Their situation is made even more difficult because they have been placed on Stage 2.3 of the Behavioural Management Program, which only allows them to make four phone calls per week, along with other harsher restrictions than the rest of us.

In response to the above restrictions, which are oppressive and deny our most basic human rights, all 13 of us are protesting in some or all of the following ways:

- *Hunger strike*
- *Remaining locked in our cell – 24-hour lockdown – not accepting the short period we have access to sunlight in our individual yards or association times with other inmates*
- *Refusing to be locked in our cell at the end of the day and staying stationary in view of the CCTV camera until carried or escorted*

- *Refusing to have visits from family or friends.*

We did not do anything to deserve any of this harsh treatment; on the contrary, the long-timers among us have been on the highest stage of the Behavioural Management Program for years waiting for exit from Supermax to general population, and the remand inmates should be regarded as 'innocent until proven guilty'.

I am also writing to protest against the defamatory allegations made against us in the media (namely newspapers such as the Australian *and the* Daily Telegraph*) following the prison's decision to allow media personnel into our unit to take pictures and video footage of us without our permission. What ensued was the publication of a number of lies and outrageous claims about us that have caused further undue stress to both inmates and their families.*

Firstly, it is quite disturbing that the Department of Corrective Services would allow media personnel access to the prison to cover a story yet continue to deny access to independent bodies who wished to investigate concerns over the inhumane treatment of prisoners. Several years ago, former Greens MP Lee Rhiannon was repeatedly refused entry into Supermax when she accompanied Human Rights groups that were investigating claims of Human Rights abuses and complaints about the oppressive treatment of prisoners in the High-Risk Management Unit. Ms Rhiannon was a fierce critic of the Goulburn Supermax prison and campaigned about the injustices and corrupt system.

In the Daily Telegraph *in March 2015, a double-page article mentions the new EHRR restrictions concerning all thirteen AA inmates. At the bottom of the page is an article titled 'Prison crackdown on radicals as inmates get IS tattoos and share beheading videos'.*

Firstly, the comment 'on February 14 Corrective Services officers discovered a mobile with an SD card on an inmate in Goulburn jail with video of beheadings'. We AA inmates are not in Goulburn jail, we are in the Supermax, a completely separate facility. This 'discovery' has absolutely nothing to do with us. This link and the dramatised suspicions and accusations are further exacerbated by the next slanderous comment a few paragraphs later: 'Suspicions that convicted terrorists were using coded messages to plot jihad from inside Goulburn's Supermax'. These are complete lies against us; no authority has ever questioned any of us over this conjecture.

To the right of the article is a green-coloured text box with an internet link reading: 'Video: Escorting a High-Risk Prisoner inside Goulburn Supermax'. Following that link, one will be able to see the video, which shows an inmate wearing orange overalls being escorted through the unit.

This is what really happened:

On the day that this footage was filmed, the General Manager (G.M.) came to the inmate's cell whilst accompanied by the camera crew and told the inmate he was going to be filmed by the media. He was made to wear the orange overalls and shackled. The inmate protested about it, but the G.M. told him that his permission wasn't required and that they had the right to take footage of him. It is worth noting that the footage was simply of him being transferred from one unit to another. This has never happened and I personally watched the camera crew, consisting of two people, follow the inmate into our unit while escorted by prison officers.

Another point worth noting is the way in which this inmate was treated leading up to this incident. In normal circumstances, a new remand inmate is held in a unit called 'Unit 7' for assessment. The inmate in question was told by the G.M. he'd only be there for seven days then be transferred to our Unit 9. However, he was kept in there for nine or ten days and coincidentally, at the precise time the officers came to escort him on a two-minute walk to Unit 9, the camera crew were conveniently right there at his cell door to film the transfer.

All this happened ten days before the news broke about the new restrictions.

A day or two after the footage was taken, the G.M. came to our unit block, took the inmate to the interview room and attempted to persuade him to sign a handwritten faxed consent form for his permission to air the footage on the media. He refused to sign and expressed his opposition to any such material of him being used in the media.

Finally, the main content of this March 8 article was about the new EHRR restrictions being in effect as of that day. We, the AA inmates who the new restrictions were made for, did not know anything about it until the G.M. saw us one by one the following day (Monday, 9 March 2015) and formally told us about the new security classification. On the Sunday, 8 March, while Australians were reading about the new laws at their breakfast tables, the prison was in full lockdown and was being turned upside down with searches and seizures of all our cells and property, including our legal briefs and documents that are supposed to be protected by Legal Privilege and, up to March 2015, many items have yet to be returned.

The Department of Corrective Services has since published on their website a number of corrections to the above lies printed in the media. However, this does not erase the undue suffering and slander both the inmates and their families have had to endure as a result of this collaboration between the DCC and the media. It is unfair for inmates to be treated as worthless media fodder and manipulated into being filmed against their will.

On the front page of the Australian *on 27 January 2015, an article was published about the inmates convicted during 'Operation Pendennis' in 2005 with the heading, 'Convicts lead new generation down path of terror'. The article alleges that 'extremists targeted by Operation Appleby, and Islamic State devotees' are visiting us in prison, which is an outright lie. Visiting procedures here are so strict that for the first few months we were restricted to non-contact visits only with our family members. It wasn't until at least six years later that one of us was allowed one friend to visit. To date, some of us are still waiting for siblings to be approved. One of us waited eight years until his brother's visits were changed from non-contact to contact visitor approved. Also, in over nine years of being here, many of our visitors have been changed back* to non-contact and then back and forth between the two categories, and others have been banned for months with no explanation given other than 'intelligence information and security reasons'.

Out of all of us, there are only two or three who have one or two non-family visitors approved and only recently. They have visited no more than one can count on one hand, and they have absolutely nothing to do with 'Operation Appleby' and are the furthest from being 'Islamic State devotees'.

We challenge the authorities to provide as little as a shred of evidence that any of us 'influential' persons are 'Islamic State supporters' or 'devotees' and one name of any visitor of ours that is linked to the 'Operation Appleby' arrests or investigation.

Another fallacious quote from the same article states that 'Authorities are alarmed by the growing influence'. To have influence in the context used in the article would require us to have contact or communication with others;

- We never exit this jail to have contact with anyone.
- Any person we wish to call requires an application form with their details; rigorous security background checks are made with the relevant authorities before any application is approved or not. All calls are monitored (live), recorded and terminated at the officer's discretion at any time. The jail phone system allows a maximum of nine preset numbers per inmate. We only have the numbers of our wives, parents and one or two siblings or friends.
- Mail – the policy for us is that all mail – sent or receiving – must be read by the intelligence department, photocopied,

inspected then approved or not for sending or receiving and confiscated without explanation at their discretion.

• *Other inmates in jail – firstly, we are all in what the court has defined as segregated custody, also known as isolation. To be allowed to have contact with another person requires a form to be filled out, called an 'Association Form'. This form has the names of the two inmates who wish to associate. It is then sent to the intelligence dept., Security Manager and the General Manager. If the application is approved, we are only ever allowed to associate with one person at a time in a designated room or area e.g. a caged room or an outside caged space approx. 10m x 10m in size, for approximately one and a half hours a day. That is, if it isn't a 'lockdown' or the designated areas are 'available'. We are only allowed a certain number of approved associates on our file at one time, depending on what stage of the Behavioural Management Program we are on.*

The bottom line is, we have almost zero contact with anyone by phone, mail or in person, and everything we do is monitored and blocked if authorities here choose. So how can it be claimed that we 'influence' anyone?

The article also claims that we are in Goulburn Maximum Security Jail. This is incorrect. We are in Supermax, known as High-Risk Maximum Correctional Centre.

Another baseless claim is that 'one of the most influential figures in the Goulburn jail is said to be Elomar'. The rebuttal is the same detail as above, but there's something else to add here; all of us six inmates from 'Operation

Pendennis' have been here for over nine years and have progressed to the highest stage of the prison's Behavioural Management Program, which is supposed to entitle us out to general population prison life. We have sat on this stage for years and watched other inmates who assault and abuse officers, break property, throw faeces on walls and the like, be given exit to general population while we are still waiting. Of all of us, Elomar has been on the highest stage of level three for the longest period of time; almost four years. This stage is only acquired by complying with the jail's rules that aim at 'maintaining good order and security'. These facts render the article's comments as nothing but slanderous lies.

I swear that the above is true and correct. Due to the fact that a number of inmates (including myself) are currently refusing meals as part of a hunger strike to protest against our unjust treatment, I sincerely request that a review of this complaint is undertaken as a matter of urgency.

The letter was written on behalf of all 13 AA inmates convicted of serious terror offences. Are they being treated harshly or fairly, given the series nature of their crimes?

That's up to you to decide . . . .

8

SMUGGLING AND ESCAPES

Goulburn, Lithgow, Kempsey and Cessnock

Phones and Poo-holes

Ring! Ring!

The infamous Supermax inmate pretended not to hear it.

Ring! Ring!

Again, he didn't acknowledge the muffled noise as three HRMU officers stood in his cell.

'He didn't look real comfy,' recalled an unnamed officer. 'He tried to keep a straight face but he was wriggling a bit.'

Ring! Ring!

Still he pretended, attempting to disguise the noise as a fart, bucking his hip to the left like a baby bronco.

'What?' he asked. 'What are you standing here for?'

Isn't that obvious, Bassam? You should have at least turned it off before you stuck it up your bum. Even just on silent. You could have even left it on vibrate, if that's your thing.

Incredibly, hilariously and *completely* true, Brothers 4 Life founder Bassam Hamzy was standing in a cell at the HRMU with a ringing, vibrating phone stuck up his arse.

Remember, this is Hamzy – the man made famous for running a deadly drug-dealing gang from his Lithgow cell with a series of smuggled mobile phones. He made almost 400 calls a day, ordering hits, bashings and drive-bys. And here he is in Supermax, the place he was sent to after being busted with mobiles . . . with a phone ringing in his arse.

Ring! Ring!

Hamzy couldn't pass off the bright trill of the phone as a fart. And no matter how much he denied having anything stuck up his bum, he knew he would soon be upended. Even if they didn't grab him by his feet and swing him in the air, or strip him nude and make him touch his toes while another officer looked into his anus, he would be kept in a room with the mobile phone still firmly lodged. And they would keep him there for as long as they wanted. And they would ring, ring and ring some more.

'They rang it just before they entered his cell,' the officer said. 'And it started ringing! They couldn't believe he'd left it on. They watched him wriggling and squirming as it rung, it was so uncomfortable for him. He looked like he was in a fair bit of pain.'

As you would be . . .

'They were watching him during a visit,' the officer said. 'Maybe it was an interview . . . I'm not sure. Anyway, they saw him slip the phone down his front before working it around into his arse. He looked so awkward sitting in a plastic chair, wiggling about, trying to slip it into his arsehole.'

Intelligence agencies had been tipped off about the phone. They knew it was coming and that it was going to be given to Hamzy.

They also had the phone number.

'They followed him out of the visit [or interview],' the officer said. 'They cracked the cell as soon as he entered it, but not as quickly as they would have liked because of the six storage tubs of legal briefs he had piled up against his door. A couple went in and another one stood just outside and rang the number.'

Yep . . . *Ring! Ring!*

'It started going off. And by the looks of him, it was vibrating too.'

Hamzy knew he was done. And the last thing he needed was another charge relating to the possession of a mobile phone while locked up in prison.

'They got it out of him,' the officer continued. 'But he reacted quickly and, after a struggle, he managed to flush it down the toilet.'

Hamzy is not the only prisoner to have unsuccessfully attempted – or succeeded – in bringing a mobile phone into the HRMU at Goulburn, Australia's highest level security jail.

'I've taken phones off inmates in Supermax,' admitted another Goulburn officer. 'They would get the phone through by having it passed to them at the MRRC [Silverwater] before shoving it up their arses. We got one, a very high-profile inmate, with one in his arse only three or four months ago [October 2015]. He went on an escort out of the HRMU, and the security wasn't as good as it should have been.'

The mobile phones that are smuggled into prison are minuscule . . . nothing like an iPhone or Samsung Galaxy. One of the smallest mobile phones in the world is a Willcom WX06A. It measures 32mm by 70mm and is just 10.7mm wide. It weighs just 32 grams.

'They are bloody small,' the officer said. 'About the size of a key ring. Inmates get strip searched and things get X-rayed, but there's only so much you can do when someone has something up their arse and it weighs less than a DVD.

'If you suspect that they have one, then you can put them in an observation cell for a while and apply some pressure, but there are no guarantees. It depends how staunch they are and how strong the muscles are in their arse.'

In a stunning coincidence, a man who was suspected of being an accessory to an attempted murder of Hamzy's aunt, Maha Hamze, which left her with multiple gunshot wounds to her legs, was also caught with a phone this year.

Bilal Haouchar, 26, was arrested in a swoop at Hope Island, along with a senior Comanchero bikie, and appeared in Lithgow court on 1 July 2013, charged with using a firearm with intent and shooting a firearm at a dwelling with reckless disregard for safety.

'Bilal Haouchar was a guy they recently busted,' the guard said. 'I can't tell you much because it was very hush-hush and way over my head. Let's just say we were listening to it. He had to use it at some stage. You would be surprised how shifty the feds and the police are. Anyway, we got him with one.'

Goldie Atkinson, Hamzy's former associate and Brothers 4 Life co-founder, revealed how phones were smuggled into facilities like Goulburn's Supermax. The reformed enforcer said the easiest way was to have the mobile 'slipped to you while out on an escort'.

An 'escort' is when a prisoner is accompanied by specially trained prison officers to another jail, a court appearance, and now – more frequently and secretly – to the NSW Crime Commission to give information to police.

'They say they're going to court, but most of the time they're going to do deals with the cops,' Atkinson said. 'But anyway, whatever the escort is, that's when you get the phones.'

Atkinson said phones would be passed around in holding cells and segregation cells while out on an escort.

'Inmates go to other jails and sit in segro,' he said. 'They will pass on messages, and then the next thing you know a phone will come into that cell. They will use it and then stick it up their arse to take back to Goulburn.

'You can also get them when you go to court and other places where security isn't so tight. It's pretty easy to get something into Supermax. Plenty of blokes have had phones, and there are guys in there with them now.'

Considering his history with Hamzy's phones – albeit being on the receiving end of the calls he made from his cell – Goldie steered clear of mobiles while in prison.

'I didn't go near any phones while I was in jail,' Atkinson said. 'I could have got one easily, and I had plenty offered to me. But given what I knew about Bas and how they can listen in on calls, I didn't want to be associated with any more conspiracy theories.'

Atkinson said that, while he had never received a call from an inmate locked up in Supermax, he was in a cell when someone next to him was speaking on a phone to a prisoner in Supermax.

Blocking and the BOSS

Meet the BOSS . . . the NSW Department of Corrective Services's latest and greatest gadget that promises to stop blokes like Hamzy from bringing phones into prison via bum.

Costing a cool 17K, the Body Orifice Security Scanner (BOSS) is a frontline weapon in the fight against inmates using mobile phones in their cells to order hits, do drug deals . . . or just update their Facebook page.

Yep . . . that happens. Heaps.

In addition to a nine-month mobile-phone blocking trial that began in Lithgow Jail on 23 September 2013 at a cost of $1.06 million – before being extended by three months and then another *three years* – a BOSS II is now being used in Goulburn Jail.

'Mobile phones are a threat to the security of prisons, and we take a zero-tolerance approach to them,' said Minister for Corrections David Elliott. 'The BOSS chair is currently being used by Western Australia and Queensland Corrections and will contribute to a safer environment for officers and inmates here at Goulburn.'

Corrections Services Commissioner Peter Severin also praised the chair and its ability to detect 'a piece of metal the size of a staple'.

'The problem is that mobile phones are getting smaller all the time,' Severin said. 'That makes them easier to hide in the body orifice . . . As inmates become smarter, we have to get smarter too.'

Sold by a company called xēkü, the 'scan zones' are described on their website as 'oral, abdominal, anal/vaginal, lower legs and feet'. The oversized chair is 127cm tall, 55cm wide and weighs 174 kilos. Inmates suspected of carrying a phone, a shiv or anything that may contain metal are placed in the chair and an alarm goes off if anything is found.

Sounds great . . .

'Yeah, but it doesn't work,' said a Goulburn officer. 'Look, it has picked up some phones, but most still get through.'

Why? Can't this thing pick up metal the size of a staple?

'Most of the phones they bring in have no metal in them,' the officer continued. 'Next to no metal, anyway. Companies, mostly Chinese, are producing phones almost exclusively to be smuggled into prisons.'

Yep . . . check this out. An item listed on Ebay.com.au:

The Zanco fly phone – white – world's smallest phone,
voice, charger, 100% plastic.
Condition: Brand New
Model: The Dot
Network: All but 3G
Weight: 21g
Dimensions: 71.8mm x 23.5mm x 13mm
Material: 100 per cent plastic
Price: AU $47.15

Forget the price, just remember that it's *100% plastic*. What good is a $17,000 metal detector, brought in to stop blokes like Bassam Hamsy from bringing in phones, when they are now making 'fobs' and 'mobs' without using metal?

'I know some guys who have been on the committee for testing the mobile phone detecting units,' said a Goulburn officer. 'Any high-profile inmate or risk to national security or high-risk inmate . . . we sit them in this chair. It's basically a metal detector.'

So does it work?

'I would say no, it doesn't work. It has picked up some phones, yeah, it has. It will pick up the types of phones you or I would use – they are full of metal parts. But the problem is that companies are coming out with new phones that are almost completely made of plastic.'

Yep. Zanco. Tiny. Light. And 100% plastic.

'The fob keys only have one metal part in them,' the officer continued. 'And that is the speaker. And the BOSS doesn't pick it up because it admits fuck-all charge. They've done many tests, and the only things they pick up are the types of phones you get in a Telstra shop. They don't pick up the Chinese-made shit; the smart cunts have made these phones exclusively to be smuggled into prison. For us, it's an impossible situation. We do our best, but the technology we get will never stop it. They are always one step ahead.'

Jamming?

Corrective Services NSW is hoping that phone jamming will provide the ultimate solution to the ever-increasing problem of illegal prison phones. The Australian Communications and Media Authority (ACMA) granted CSNSW an exemption from Australia's *Radio Communications Act 1992* – which makes it an offence to operate, supply or possess jamming devices – to allow the trial to begin.

Lithgow Jail was chosen to conduct the six-month trial, and a series of antennae, capable of blocking mobile phone signals, were erected throughout the jail.

'In the past five years, we have significantly stepped up efforts to seize and detect mobile phones in our centres and have removed hundreds of mobile phones and accessories from circulation,' said Commissioner Severin when the trial commenced. 'However, inmates continue to try new and devious ways to obtain them.

'We believe this jamming technology is the ultimate answer, because even if an inmate does obtain a mobile phone, it will be worthless because it won't work.'

Little to no information was publicly released at the conclusion of the trial. On 9 July 2014, Minister for Justice

Brad Hazzard issued a media release stating the trial had been extended for another three months: 'Corrective Services NSW has been making headway against contraband in prisoners with targeted deterrence and detection, which has resulted in more seizures of contraband, including mobile phones. Jamming means inmates can no longer thumb their nose at the system, and the contraband value of a mobile phone becomes worthless.'

Okay. Great. So end the trial and roll it out. Put it in every prison in Australia.

The release continued: 'More than 91,000 searches inside prisons by CSNSW Security Operations Group and sniffer dogs in 2013 resulted in a 440 per cent increase in mobile phone seizures – from 39 in 2009 to 211 in 2013.'

But what's that got to do with phone jamming?

The nine-month trial, extended to a year, was then extended by another *four* years and will end on 1 November 2018.

Why?

'Because it doesn't work at all,' another officer said. 'Don't even bother asking me about it. It does not work at all. It's a fucking disgrace. At Lithgow [during the first stage of the trial], we busted blokes standing in the middle of the yard talking on phones. We confiscated them. It's impossible to jam the signal in every area of the jail with affecting areas outside of the jail. It just doesn't work.'

A letter obtained from ACMA to ACT Minister for Justice Shane Rattenbury argued that the trial at Lithgow had been a success and called on the ACT to participate in a similar trial. Here is an edited transcript of the letter, signed by David Brumfield, Executive Manager, Spectrum Management Policy Branch:

In July 2013 the ACMA implemented the necessary legislative and regulatory oversight arrangements to enable a trial of mobile phone jammers at Lithgow Correctional Centre, New South Wales (Lithgow). The formal period of the Lithgow trial was completed on 22 January 2015 with the submission of a report by Corrective Services New South Wales (CSNSW) setting out the findings of the trial. The ACMA has determined that the Lithgow trial has been successful in establishing that the operation of a jammer at this location can render mobile phones mostly inoperable within the confines of the facility, while avoiding interference to critical radio communications networks (such as those used for public mobile telephony) beyond the perimeter of the facility. With this in mind, the ACMA has agreed to a three-year extension to the Lithgow trial, and is in the process of finalising the necessary legislation for this extension.

The ACMA has also agreed to a similar trial at a correctional facility in a more densely populated area in NSW, at the request of CSNSW. This will allow the ACMA to assess the interference risk of a mobile phone jammer in operation in a medium-density area, and will contribute to the development of a measured, risk-based policy on the wider deployment of mobile phone jammers in correctional facilities. The ACMA is considering Goulburn for this trial.'

In this letter, the ACMA admits the technology 'can render mobile phones *mostly* inoperable'. This admission means inmates are still finding a way to beat the system. The letter also reveals Goulburn, 'a more densely populated area', will host a similar trial.

'Talk of extending it to Goulburn is just ridiculous,' the officer continued. 'I can tell you right now there isn't one [jamming device] in Goulburn. And they won't be able to put one in. Not at all. It would ruin the signal for the local community. There's a primary school and a bunch of businesses, like the smash repair right across the road, that would be affected. They can't do it. It's a complete waste of money.'

In the letter, the ACMA declares they have 'developed the following criteria for correctional centres to be a potential site for a mobile phone jammer trial':

1. *500 metres or greater from major roads, residences or businesses; and*
2. *1 kilometre or greater from the nearest transmitter site used to supply mobile phone networks.*

Well, guess what? Goulburn North Public School is only 400 metres away from Goulburn Correctional Centre. Goulburn Tyremasters? Just 200 metres away. Pro State Exhausts? It's directly across the road – no more than 100 metres away.

In fact, nearly every business on Maud Street, William Street, and even some in Wayo Street – and there are many – are well within the 500 metres the ACMA has said would rule the jamming technology ineligible. It appears they will be breaking their own criteria should a jamming trial be approved at Goulburn.

Corrective Services said they were seeking approval from the ACMA when approached for comment.

'Mobile phone jamming started under Commissioner Peter Severin, an Australian first,' said a spokesman. 'Following a successful trial at Lithgow Correctional Centre, CSNSW is seeking approval from the Australian Communications and Media Authority to increase the use of jamming, including at Goulburn Correctional Centre.'

The ACT have so far rejected approaches to trial the jamming technology in their prisons because they also breach the distance requirement from the road and the proximity to businesses.

ACT opposition spokesman Andrew Wall is the only person on record to speak sense on the issue. Wall said the government should adopt more than one approach to stopping mobile phones from being smuggled into jails. He also said jamming technology should be secondary to people power:

'There's limited ways contraband can enter, so we need to identify how it is getting in and what can be done to stop that. The government needs to look at the weaknesses in the existing system to identify where the flaws are and what can be done to address them.

'[They should] look at what is best practice elsewhere, both in Australia and jurisdictions overseas, to work out what practices can be adopted to stop the contraband coming in and then render it useless if it does enter.

'If you don't fix the problem, it will continue to be a problem.'

Holy Smokes!

1. Take the nicotine patch – the one of many handed to inmates for free during the three-month 'nicotine replacement amnesty' – and peel back the hard plastic to reveal the sticky coating on the underside of the patch.
2. Fill the kettle with water and boil.
3. Pour a small amount of boiling water into a cup.
4. Place the patch into the cup.
5. Wait until all the nicotine paste on the underside of the patch dissolves into the boiling water.
6. Place tea leaves, removed from a Lipton's bag, into the nicotine-soaked water.
7. Leave tea leaves soaking in water (for an hour) and then remove.
8. Allow the tea leaves to dry, heat under lit flames if necessary.
9. Rip an onion page from a holy book.
10. Place nicotine-soaked tea leaves into the page.
11. Roll.
12. Smoke.

The riot squads were ready. The prisons were set to explode.

Every emergency response unit in the prison system was put on standby after Corrective Services NSW announced that a state-wide ban on cigarettes in prison would be rolled out in August 2015 following trials in Lithgow and the maximum-security wing at Cessnock Jail.

'We thought they were going to go off,' said an officer who was sent to Goulburn when the smoking ban was introduced at the notorious jail. 'But they didn't.'

Nothing happened. The inmates did not fight, kick, scream or beg. There were no meltdowns or tantrums.

Not yet . . .

'They all got patches for free at the beginning,' the officer continued. 'And to be honest, they worked fine. A lot of them seemed happy to be giving cigarettes up. I think you'll find that most smokers want to quit but just can't find the will-power. And smokes were costing them about $30 a pack [$28 on a prison 'buy-up' list obtained before the ban was announced]. And they were fine with quitting.'

For a while . . .

And that's because many of the 'former smokers' were still smoking.

'They started smoking tea leaves with nicotine patches in them,' said a guard.

'It was the worst smell ever. They'd roll the patches up and put the tea leaves inside. They'd make it real hot and suck on the fumes.'

Others found a more discreet way to make smokes.

'You could smell the burning plastic and they were getting busted,' the officer continued. 'So that's when they started boiling the nicotine out of the patches and soaking them into the tea leaves.'

Brett Collins, a former inmate who is now a prisoners' rights activist, said the smoking bans were denying the inmates a human right. He also revealed that nicotine lozenges were soon the inmate's preferred choice of replacement therapy.

'We get hundreds of letters from the prisoners, complaining about the bans,' Collins said. 'One was saying that the preferred way of getting around it was to use lozenges instead of patches, as they can easily be melted down and put into the tea leaves.

'People are so bored that ways of getting around the system are all part of the entertainment. You end up causing tension, and people get creative and work around the problem. It's an outrageous way of making them use their energy. We try to get them to use their time positively, but it's hard.

'The smoking issue is one that is very important to people, because 85 per cent of the prison population smokes. [The Cancer Council reports that the rate of smoking in prison is five times higher than the New South Wales general population.] It's a human rights issue, and it's totally wrong to stop them from smoking. That doesn't mean we don't disagree that smoking is a health problem and an issue that needs to be addressed, but we would rather give them a program to quit rather than force them to.'

So all was quite. Some stuck the patches on their arms, others cut them up and smoked them. There were no riots and few complaints.

And then the shit hit the fan.

The inmates were soon told they had to buy their own patches. The department would no longer hand them out for free – with the exception of new receptions – given the replacement therapy should have weaned them off nicotine.

Tobacco became the prison system's newest and most expensive illegal drug.

'The smoking wasn't an issue, but it is now,' another officer said. 'It has taken this long for it to become a problem. And it's a big problem. They are getting restless, they are in the yard all day missing it. They need that nicotine. The patch is starting to die out because they can't afford to buy them. The amnesty is over and we don't have to provide them with patches anymore. They got three months and that was it. Everything was okay when they were on the patches. There was no trouble. We were waiting every day for the prison to explode, but it was fine. Now, well, that's a different story.'

Inmates are paying up to $600 for a pouch of tobacco, according to some. A $2.50 BIC lighter – a gas-filled piece of plastic with a flint? $90. Papers? $50.

'Tobacco is now worth more than any other drug,' the officer continued. 'It's so hard to get in. They're going nuts. At first they hoarded it all, but now they have to smuggle it in. They were paying up to $300 for a pack of smokes, which came from the blokes who'd stocked up. Now it's tobacco they buy, because they can't really put a pack of Winfield Reds up their arses. They buy tobacco that's been smuggled in – wrapped up in Glad Wrap or condoms like any other drug. Ten grams of tobacco, which is pretty much the standard, is going for $100. That's what they're paying. It is gold. If you have an ounce of tobacco, it's worth $500. Nine times out of ten they'll smuggle in a lighter and papers with the tobacco. Flint or matches. It will be a couple of balloons with all the different things in them. Every day at visits or a ramp, you'll find a lighter or matches. You find them everywhere. It's pretty hard to catch someone with a match up the arse. We don't have the resources to police it. I mean, you can smell the smoke everywhere in the prison. The guys getting it in are the head honchos now, and they are becoming very powerful.'

And the violence has begun.

'People are being bashed and stabbed over tobacco,' another officer said. 'Inmates are failing to pay their tobacco debts. They are chalking up debts and getting hits put on them when they don't pay up. If you don't pay your debt, you're going to get bashed. It happens all the time. Someone will be killed over it soon.'

The *Sydney Morning Herald* reported one of the first acts of violence in relation to the smoking bans. According to one of the prisoners, a brawl broke out in Cooma Correctional Centre when inmates were scavenging to retrieve cigarette butts or 'bumpers'.

He said a group of industrious men had attached sticky tape to the end of a one-metre-long TV coaxial cable and were probing the 20-millimetre hole filled with old bumpers.

'Word soon spread around the prison that there was loads of vintage tobacco . . . The fight started after several inmates were heard arguing that they had disposed of bumpers down the hole, [so] the bumpers should be divided equally,' the inmate told the *Herald*. 'Things only escalated when the inmate with the probing tool refused to share his invention.'

The prisoner said some inmates had armed themselves with plastic knives and were digging tobacco from cracks.

A current inmate in the maximum-security wing at Cessnock Jail said new inmates were being bashed for patches.

'They are the only guys who get it for free,' the inmate said. 'When they come in they are issued patches for nothing, to give them time to beat their addiction. But that just makes them a target. They get stood over straightaway for their patches, and they are bashed or stabbed if they don't give them up.'

A guard from the same jail said officers were now concerned for their own safety as inmates become 'edgy' due to the side effects associated with nicotine withdrawal.

'It was brought in by the department because it was a workplace safety issue for us,' the officer continued. 'Well, I would rather breathe in a bit of smoke than be stabbed in the back by some lunatic who goes nuts because he can't get a smoke. Really, they could have made smoking areas like they have in pubs and paid those officers who patrolled that area more money for the risk. A lot of officers smoke, and it wouldn't have worried them a bit.

'It just comes down to manpower, and they would rather ban it and put us at risk rather than hire the staff needed to patrol it.'

Officers are regularly making 'tobacco busts'.

'We got a bloke recently who smuggled in two lots of

ten grams,' an officer said. 'That was in September. He was asking 500 bucks for it. His sheila had carried it in in her mutt [vagina], and she pulled it out in the visit. It went into a packet of chips, and we saw him putting it down his overalls before working it into his arse. We saw it on camera, went and searched him, and got it hanging out of his arse. It was in two balloons. They do smuggle in flints and matches and all that, but this bloke just had tobacco.

'He was sore and sorry, and we just looked at him and said, "How stupid are you?" We had to upend him and use force. It's the same thing as bringing in a drug like ice and carries the same charge. But they'll do it because there's a market for it.'

According to another officer, the police are not taking the issue seriously. Here is how a call to a police station was described following a tobacco find.

'Hi, constable. We've seized a large quantity of contraband. Could you come down and charge the prisoner?'

'Sure, what we got? Smack? Ice?'

'Tobacco.'

The constable laughed. 'Mate, we aren't coming down for that!'

Click. End of call.

'We're putting a lot of resources into it,' the officer said. 'We have cell searches and we're patrolling visits. We don't have a tobacco dog, but I think that might be in the plans. We're searching them with a normal drug dog, which isn't very effective, but we are finding it in mouths, shoes and hands. We have to treat it seriously. But the coppers don't know how to charge them properly. We're finding, say 20 grams, then we ring the cops. If it was 20 grams of ice they'd be there, charging them in a second. But with tobacco, they're like, *really*?

'We can punish them more than they or the courts can, so we're dealing with it internally. We can ban a visitor for two years, but what can the cops do for someone trying to bring it in? I'm not aware of any criminal charges, but once they work at the legislation properly there will be.

'They're trying to come to terms with it. I could go to the boss with a big score of tobacco, and he could just be like, "I don't care. Throw it out." The cops don't give a shit because it's such grey area.

'We have a battle on our hands.'

That they do . . .

Hacksaws and Holes

An infamous Melbourne criminal called 'The Runner' – the mysterious underworld figure who shot and killed Melbourne gangland figure Jason Moran before turning police inform- ant – can now be revealed as the man behind the escape that embarrassed Goulburn Jail in 2015, when an inmate scaled a fence just days after being moved into maximum security for, wait for it, trying to escape.

A Goulburn guard claims 'The Runner', whose identity was suppressed by police, and a dodgy security system helped Stephen Jamieson climb a barbwire fence to freedom on 18 August.

Leaving prison officials red-faced, Jamieson went on the run just ten days after being moved into a segregation cell for digging a hole under a cabinet in the jail's furniture workshop.

'He cut the cage of the external yard with a hacksaw blade,' the officer said. 'That was the first part. There are little cages at the back of the segregation cells, and he wouldn't have been able to escape had he not had something to cut through the cage.'

The guard claims the hacksaw blade was a gift from the former gangland warrior.

'I'm not sure how The Runner got the hacksaw blade in,' the officer said. 'He's a real shifty character and has plenty of opportunities to bring things in and out when he goes on his little trips to visit the police. Anyway, he got it in and he's the man who we believe gave it to Jamieson.'

How he got the blade, and who he got it from, isn't the embarrassing part – being able to walk unnoticed across a prison yard in broad daylight, while holding pillows, blankets and a broom handle, before scaling a gigantic razor-topped perimeter wall, is.

Corrective Services boss Peter Severin ordered an independent review of security after the 28-year-old Jamieson, serving 13 years for armed robbery, left the maximum-security prison unnoticed at about 1pm.

'There is clearly, absolutely no excuse for someone being able to escape from maximum security,' Severin said at the time. 'This is an incident that needs to be followed up very swiftly.'

The commissioner would not have liked what he was told when the investigators handed in their report.

'There are motion detection devices in that area,' the officer revealed. 'And they were playing up when Jamieson escaped. People were at first saying he was able to get out because we were understaffed following heaps of overtime and extra shifts when the smoking bans came in. But that wasn't the case. The motion detectors weren't working – if they would have been, he wouldn't have made it out.'

The high-ranking Goulburn official explained that officers monitor a series of CCTV screens in a control room.

'The motion detectors are set up on the cameras, and any movement in that area should bring the vision straight up on a screen,' he said. 'But they weren't picking up anything at the time. The guys in the control room were looking at their screens, but obviously that particular camera wasn't coming up.'

Yep, the one that would have showed the comedy routine of the green-clad criminal repeatedly trying – and failing – to throw his rope made of bedsheets over the wall.

'He actually had to have a couple of goes, because it didn't catch the first couple of times,' the officer said. 'It was quite funny watching the vision when we got it. Eventually he climbed up the rope and cut himself a few times on the way.'

Unoccupied patrol towers also contributed to the brazen daylight escape.

'He was very lucky,' the officer said. 'Even with the camera failure he would have been spotted had the two back towers been manned. The towers were only manned at night back then, which was just bloody ridiculous. They were put there for a reason. You have guys with guns on the internal perimeter, but they couldn't see. A guard in one of the towers would have spotted it straightaway.'

Stephen Jamieson was put into Supermax following his apprehension. He pleaded guilty via video link to charges of escaping lawful custody, taking conveyance without consent of owner, police pursuit, dangerous driving, being an unlicensed driver, driving an unregistered car and not being insured.

Phew! What a mouthful.

Jamieson was recaptured ten hours after he escaped at Pheasants Nest, about 100 kilometres from the prison. He was spotted driving a stolen ute and apprehended when police used road spikes to end his short time on the run following a high-speed pursuit.

Hysterically, his lawyer argued about charges relating to his licence, saying he hadn't had a chance to renew it as it expired while he was in jail.

Maybe it could have also been argued that he didn't know the car that he'd stolen was out of registration and insurance?

As for the cameras? Fixed. And the towers? Well, they are now manned . . . both day and night.

Corrective Services NSW had their own view on the Jamieson caper, with a spokesman for the department saying, 'When Stephen Jamieson escaped from Goulburn Correctional Centre, the electronic system was not malfunctioning. Two towers had not been permanently staffed for some years following a decision made by a previous commissioner. This had not been referred to Commissioner Severin as a security risk before Jamieson's escape.'

But, still, inmates find ways to get out . . .

The Shaw-Shag Redemption
28 September, 2015. 8.48pm.

'Love you, my princess,' Beau Wiles posted on Facebook. Attached was a photograph. Green hat back to front, arms folded and muscles flexing, Beau posed for his princess wearing only his cap and undies.

So what? Happens every day. Kids take pictures like this all the time and post them on Twitter, Snapchat, Instagram, Facebook . . .

Sure, but not from prison.

Wiles, a run-of-the-mill, minimum-security nobody, would soon become an infamous Australian fugitive thanks to Facebook and the mobile phone he had smuggled into his cell. The shoplifter had been using the phone to update his Facebook profile while in Goulburn.

Wiles also used the mobile to land him some love.

'Love you too, my prince,' his girlfriend, Rebecca Watts, wrote back. 'I can't wait to have my hand all ova that sexy body of urz.'

In another post: 'That's my man looking as fresh as always. Can't wait to marry you! As soon as ur out im gunna make u my husband xxxx.'

Apparently she couldn't wait. Literally.

Wiles escaped from Goulburn Jail just two days after

posting in the semi-nude. The loved-up jailbird used his mobile phone, which he is understood to have had for three weeks prior to 'vanishing', to arrange the not-so-daring escape.

'He was picked up in a black Commodore,' said NSW Minister for Corrections David Elliott after the inmate fled a minimum-security work area and jumped in the waiting car at about 10am. 'I don't know what I am more disgusted about: the way he escaped, or just the fact he's s so stupid that he's just thrown his life away. Last year we were able acquire 325 phones, but obviously we can't get all of them. What's happened in the last 24 hours is unacceptable, and we need to make sure it doesn't happen again.'

Like the jail-fence jumper Jamieson, Wiles' freedom was short-lived; he and his lover were arrested 31 hours after the escape. Wiles was picked up 160 kilometres away from Goulburn – with his gal – after being spotted by a keen-eyed officer in Unanderra, near Wollongong.

'It was just a highway stop, and police recognised him,' said Lake Illawarra Acting Inspector Matt Glasgow. 'He wasn't driving. He was in the backseat.'

Both Wiles and Rebecca Watts, a 32-year-old mother of four, were arrested. So was a 43-year-old woman and a 39-year-old-man, who were both suspected of helping the lovers plan and plot the Facebook escape.

Wiles and Watts will be forced to wait at least 16 months until they get married, after the escapee was given another six months in prison. Wiles had about ten months left to serve when he leaped into the Commodore outside the jail.

Wiles's lawyer suggested the media coverage had also served as additional punishment.

'It did attract, for some reason, a great deal of media interest,' defence solicitor Laura Fennel said. 'Forevermore, when his name is Googled, there will be a Facebook picture of him in a very unflattering pose in red underpants. It's something he'll have to live with the rest of his life.'

Wiles was sentenced to a maximum of two years with a non-parole period of six months. Watts was also given a maximum sentence of two years for her role in the escape.

9

HORRIBLE HISTORIES
Pentridge and Grafton

H is for Hell (Division)

John Reginald Killick – a much younger, stronger and far more violent version of the helicopter escapee in chapter four – smashed the guard in the head.

'I cracked him with an iron bar,' recalled Killick, who was 26 years old at the time of the attack. 'Straight in the head.'

The guard was down . . . but he wasn't out.

'So I hit him again,' Killick said. 'I made sure I'd put him to sleep.'

Smack!

The semi-conscious officer copped it right on the chin, the blow breaking his jaw and delivering him to death's door.

Yep. He was asleep alright.

Killick looked at Mac and Geoff. The two men who had plotted the escape with him were standing silent, completely stunned.

'Get the fucking keys!' Killick screamed. '*Now*. Let's go. We're out of here!'

They had already cut through the bars with a hacksaw. Killick looked down at the guard.

Is he dead? Fuck it. Time to go . . .

You already know Killick – everyone does. In 1999 his lover, Lucy, yanked him out of a maximum-security prison by helicopter in one of the world's most famous jailbreaks. But you probably don't know about his *other* attempts, including a 1968 failure that would see him spend four years of his life in the Pentridge Prison hell known as H Division. You'll probably also be surprised to learn that Killick wasn't always a gentleman. No, he wasn't always the polite, white-haired old man you might see sipping coffee on a Sunday at Milsons Point . . .

'We got the screw down on the ground,' Killick continued. 'And I smashed him over the head with an iron bar. It was ruthless and the wrong thing to do, but I was desperate. I'm lucky that I didn't kill him. I hit him front on – hard.'

But not hard enough to put prison officer John de Boer to sleep.

'He turned around so I had to hit him again,' Killick said. 'I hit him flush on the chin, and this one knocked him out.'

Killick, the bank robber busted in Melbourne, had spent weeks planning the escape. Facing at least five years in

Pentridge before being extradited to New South Wales to be trialled for two *other* armed hold-ups, he had enlisted Mac and Geoff for the three-man job.

Killick wasn't going to spend the next 20 years in jail.

'Now listen,' he'd told his fellow inmates earlier. 'Geoff, Mac and me are busting out tonight. As long as no one tries to interfere, no one will get hurt. But if anyone tries to stop us or alerts a screw . . . I'll belt your brains out with this.'

He waved the iron bar, pointing and threatening.

Killick and Co. thought they were a mugging away from freedom.

'We'd got a hacksaw blade a few days before,' Killick said. 'And we cut through bars so we could get into a dormitory. There was only one more door to go through and we needed the key.'

That's why he belted the guard. But there was one problem . . .

'No keys,' Mac said. 'He doesn't have any fucking keys!'

Killick checked. *Yep . . . no keys.*

'We thought he would have had the keys, but he didn't,' Killick said. 'They'd changed the protocol after a guy called Walker had escaped. We had no idea, and without the keys we were fucked.'

The trio screamed at each other.

'What are we going to do now?' yelled Geoff, pointing at the bloodied guard on the ground. '*WHAT THE FUCK ARE WE GOING TO DO?*'

Killick knelt beside the – *dying?* – guard and grabbed at his belt. He stood back up, holding a gun.

'This is what we're going to do,' he shouted. They walked out into the wing, to the very locked wing they didn't have keys to and, well . . . it was locked.

'Stay where you are or you're dead,' screamed a voice, amplified by a handheld PA. 'We have you surrounded.'

Killick looked across to the wounded guard and then back to the gun in his hand.

'Fuck this,' he said. 'I'm going to go down swinging.'

Mac and Geoff nodded.

'So we started a siege,' Killick said. 'We grabbed whatever we could and barricaded the place up. I had a gun and a hostage, and I was ready to go out shooting. I thought I was completely fucked and couldn't imagine any other way out.'

Killick and Co. dug in. They were ready to die.

'The jail was surrounded,' Killick said. 'They issued threats and we issued demands, but it wasn't going anywhere until the commissioner came down.'

The boss of the jail was prepared to offer them a deal, desperate to get to his dying guard.

'Okay, boys,' he said. 'We need to end this, and end it now. I know it seems hopeless, but I'm willing to offer you a one-off deal. If you surrender – let us in and hand over the gun and the guard – I can promise you that we will not issue any outside charges. You will not face court or serve any more time for what you have done here today.'

It was a start.

'But what about H Division?' Killick asked. 'You blokes will kill us for what we've done to the screw.'

The commissioner went silent . . . but he soon replied.

'Well, I can't promise that you won't be sent to H Division,' he said. 'In fact, I think that's the only place for you after this. You may be there for a very long time. But I can give you my word, my personal guarantee, that the officers will not lay a hand on you. You will never be touched.'

Really? Well, that's better than being shot.

'The deal was pretty good,' Killick said. 'We weren't going to get any more time and we weren't going to get bashed. I was prepared to go and have a shootout with them until I heard that. I was ready to die and take as many of them out as I could. I really thought I was screwed.'

The deal stopped Killick from shooting – from killing and from dying.

'Part of the deal was that I had to spend the rest of my sentence in H Division,' Killick said. 'That scared the shit out of me, but I had the boss's word I wouldn't be bashed. I knew they would still get to me somehow, for what I'd done, but right there and then it was good enough for me.'

Killick dropped the gun.

So what happened to turn Killick into a would-be killer? What had made him bash a guard, grab a gun and go, *Fuck this – I'll go down in flames*? H Division happened, that's what.

'I had already spent six months in H Division,' Killick said. 'They sent me there for trying to escape. It was nothing like the attempt I just told you about.'

Yep, no hacksaws, iron bars or guns.

'I'd tried to do a runner from court. I was bloody fast back then, and I knew if I could get in the clear that nobody was going to catch me. The screw took my handcuffs off for sentencing, and I got seven years for robbing a bank. The cops weren't there because their car had broken down, so I was left with only the two screws who took me to court. I thought, *This is my chance.*'

Yep, no police – just two fat screws.

'I came out of court and one of the screws looked at me and said, "You should be thankful you only got seven years." So I whacked him – a clean hit straight to his solar plexus. I pushed the other guy and dived out of the doors. I got down the steps and was on my way.'

Well . . . almost.

'You wouldn't believe it, but I was brought down by a textbook Rugby League tackle in a state where they've never even heard of Rugby League,' Killick said. 'They were all AFL mad, but this screw just cleaned me up in the best tackle I'd ever seen. He would have been the only bloke in Melbourne who knew how to tackle.'

Killick's punishment: six months in hell.

'I got flogged as soon as I got there,' Killick said of H Division, the infamous punishment section of Pentridge Prison. 'I walked past this big mirror, it was on my left, and then a couple of regular screws handed me over to the H Division guards. They told me to strip.'

Then they told him to walk – naked, cuffed and completely helpless.

Whack! A baton to the guts.

Killick keeled over and gasped for air.

'Keep on walking,' a screw shouted. 'Did anyone tell you to stop?'

Slap! This time a stinging slug on the arse, his white cheeks immediately welting red.

Killick winced and then took a few steps.

Crack! Baton smacking bony knee.

He was down again . . .

'Up, you maggot,' a guard yelled and spat, a different one this time.

Killick picked himself off the floor.

'I think there were three or four of them,' Killick said. 'And they smashed me up with a baton. They told me to strip, and then made me march around in a circle, cracking me as I walked by. They were screaming at me: "You weak cunt" and "You fucking scum", stuff like that. A bloke I called Hitler was the worst. He screamed and spat all over my face.'

The welcoming – all bats, blood and bruises – was known as the 'reception biff'. Each inmate who was sent to H Division was forced to walk the 'Liquorice Mile'.

'They would try and ruin you before you even got to your cell,' Killick said. 'And some blokes would break down. They would try to cut themselves, swallow things and kill themselves as soon as they got there. The screws kept on belting you until they got bored or until it was knock-off time. I think I actually copped it pretty lightly. I've spoken to plenty of others who claim to have had it far worse.'

Victoria's biggest jail, HM Prison Pentridge, opened in 1850, and a section of the compound was walled off in

1958 following a series of violent and highly embarrassing escapes. The newly created H Division was where the state's worst inmates would be housed. And they would be beaten and bashed – and most were broken . . .

'I had heard about Grafton, and I knew this was the equivalent,' Killick said. 'I wouldn't say it was *worse* than Grafton, but it was certainly its equal. I got a real savage whack the first time, and a few whacks here and there, but it was more mental torture and abuse. I could pretend that I got whacked every day but I didn't – though some blokes did. You could hear them getting belted. We all knew what was going on.'

Killick hardly saw another inmate for six months . . . The only people he saw were baton-wielding screws. He was kept in his empty cell, locked up alone all night. During the day he broke rocks, the bank robber busting the famous Pentridge bluestone that just happened to build the very walls that imprisoned him in this hell.

'I broke rocks for six months,' Killick said. 'I was sent out into a little yard and was given a hammer. I sat there all day breaking big rocks down into little rocks. You would get an hour for lunch and then be sent back out. You would break rocks all day and then return to your solitary cell. It was horrible. I looked forward to little things, like showering, which we only got three days a week: Monday, Wednesday and Friday.'

Hell Division is what turned Killick into an escapee prepared to kill. And, ironically, he would end up spending another four years in H Division because of the failed escape. Only three men ever served more time breaking rocks and copping beltings in arguably the worst punishment jail in Australia's history.

'I ended up spending a lot of time in there,' Killick said. 'And I had plenty of time to think about what I'd done. I felt terrible about belting the screw, and the only thing that made me feel any better was that he later told me that he would have shot me if he could have. I had massive regrets. It was a terrible thing to do, but I was pretty gone in the head. I was facing extradition to New South Wales for other robberies and was just desperate to get out. I can't make excuses for what I did – it's the worst thing I've done in my life. And to make it worse, the guy I hit was a *good* screw. He was one of the better blokes.'

L is for Last Man Hung

Killick was woken in the middle of the night and removed from his H Division hell. It was a day or so after he'd put down the gun and handed over the guard. As promised, he hadn't been belted or bashed – not even handled roughly. But what was to come . . . Well, he would have rather copped bats, blood and bruises.

A posse of guards stood at his door.

'Out, Killick!' they yelled. 'Something has happened. You need to come with us *now*.'

They waited for him to rise and then walked him – no one pushing or prodding – to another wing.

Shit. This is good. Out of H Division already?

'They marched me out of the block,' Killick recalled. 'I didn't know what was happening.'

The officers suddenly stopped.

'Here,' one of them said, pointing into the darkness. 'This is your new home.'

Killick was standing in front of the cell last used by Ronald Ryan – the last man in Australia to be legally executed by hanging.

'It was the condemned cell,' Killick said. 'It was the place Ryan had been kept in while he waited on death row.'

The guards nodded at Killick, the shock having sent him an iridescent shade of white.

'Yeah, mate,' one said. 'You're next. You just signed your own death warrant. Bad luck, buddy.'

What?

'They told me I was going to get the death penalty,' Killick said. 'They told me the officer I'd hit had died that afternoon. They told me I would be charged with murder and I would hang.'

Oh shit. I'm screwed.

'You can only imagine the trauma. I was in a bad way. I spent the first night thinking I would soon be dead, that I would suffer the same fate as old Ron.'

Killick had known Ryan, and he'll never forget the date of his hanging: 3-2-1967.

'It was absolutely horrible,' Killick said. 'It was something everyone in the prison went through. No one wanted him to die, not even the guards.

'They gave him a 48-hour reprieve because there was talk

that he could be proved innocent,' Killick said, remembering the cheers, however hollow they sounded. 'The whole prison erupted in joy when we were told. We all shouted and cheered. We were hopeful that he would live.'

But then the governor came to break the news, individually stopping at each cell.

'The night before Ron was eventually executed, the governor came round with tears in his eyes,' Killick recalled. 'And he told us that he'd spoken to Ron, and he had accepted his fate. He told us the decision had been made and Ron was going to die. He said that Ron had told him to tell us all not to play up, because it wouldn't do anyone any good. As a favour to Ron, we should just accept it.'

So the inmates remained quiet, and on the morning of 3 February 1967, they slowly collected their breakfast before silently returning to their cells.

'We all turned on our radios and waited,' Killick said. 'And at about five minutes past eight it was announced: he was dead. Hung.'

Ronald Ryan was dropped from the gallows at exactly 8am. The rope that had been meticulously measured to 7 feet – allowing for Ryan's body weight and height – was let loose by the hangman, an unknown officer who wore a grey suit, welder's goggles and a green cloth cap over his head. Ryan's neck snapped when the rope wound out, the drop measured to perfection. He wasn't decapitated or left to strangle. Ryan was pronounced dead at 8.04am.

Sentenced to hang for murdering 41-year-old prison officer George Hodson during an escape from Pentridge with fellow inmate Peter Walker, Ryan was dumped in an unmark grave with the nine other men executed in Pentridge and another 99 who had been moved from Old Melbourne Gaol. He was laid to rest next to Ned Kelly (minus the famous bushranger's skull).

'And I thought I was next,' said Killick. 'I didn't know the death penalty was about to be abolished, and I sat there thinking I would be hung, just like Ron.'

But after two days he had a light-bulb moment.

'The police had not come,' Killick said. 'Surely they would have wanted to interview me if this was murder and the guard was dead.'

Yep . . . it was just a joke. A sick and twisted way for the officers of Pentridge to inflict hurt on Killick without leaving him scared – at least physically.

'I was there for 48 hours, and they came in on Sunday night and told me the officer had made a remarkable recovery. What pricks . . .'

Ronald Ryan was to remain the last man executed in Australia.

F is for Flogged

Killick was minding his own business, just sitting and looking at his cards. It was a good hand – queens and aces.

'You're not king of the yard!'

He didn't have time to react to the cry rushing towards him or to the man who had issued the threat, all cocked arms coming for him.

Whack!

The blow knocked him off his seat, sending his queens and aces into the air.

He looked up towards his attacker.

William O'Meally, regarded by some as the toughest man ever to have been locked up in Pentridge, was standing over him, puffing, panting, ready to pounce.

'I was eventually put into a yard with O'Meally,' Killick said. 'It was a yard full of heavies – the Russell Street bomber was one of them. Peter Walker was there too. Walker shook my hand first, and then O'Meally – a real strong grip – and he said, "You know you did the wrong thing, don't you?" I looked at him and said, "What do you mean?" He told me that my escape attempt had affected all of the other prisoners, especially him, with security being tightened.

'Anyway, he told me that he was due out, but because of me he was going to do another two years. He told me it set him back and it was my fault. That was bullshit. I just walked away and knew I would have to watch him.'

Whack!

O'Meally struck again, but Killick saw it coming and blocked the blow, jumping to his feet.

'I was pretty fit, and so was he,' Killick said. 'But I was only 26 and he was 49. Anyway, we got into it and were going for about five or six minutes. I ended up getting him and had him in the corner. I was whacking the shit out of him, and next thing – *bang!* I thought he had gotten one in, but it was the screws with the firehose. They sent us both flying and separated us before I could finish him.'

O'Meally was deflated by the near-beating. The jail's toughest man had almost been knocked out by a kid.

'They put us back in the same yard and we shook hands,' Killick said. 'I knew he was never sweet with me, but we got on because we had to. He was almost broken by then, and eventually would be, turning to the Bible.'

William John O'Meally, born 20 November 1920, holds the record for spending the most time in H Division. He did a staggering 11 years in the house of horrors, breaking rocks and being bashed with batons. He was given the death sentence for killing a police officer, but had the punishment overturned to 'life' after spending two years on death row.

He'd shot an officer in the leg during an escape attempt that led, not only to H Division being created, but also to a famous flogging. O'Meally was sentenced to 12 lashings for shooting the officer, and he would go down in history as the last man in Australia to be legally flogged.

'Your hands are lifted above your head and you are shackled to the triangle,' O'Meally said after he was released in 1989. 'When you get hit with the first stroke, it explodes within you. It strips the skin from you and you feel like you are in another world. By the time the twelfth stroke has been reached, you are in a state of delirium. You bite your tongue, you vomit, and you can see blood and bits of flesh around you.'

O'Meally wasn't exaggerating the ordeal; the scars were there for all to see.

'He used to whine about it all the time,' Killick said. 'And it was his claim to fame in a way. He would tell everyone how terrible it was and used to show us the scars. They were bloody horrible and he obviously went through a lot. The scars were quite pronounced. He told us they threw him down on this triangle and stretched him out. Then they flogged him half dead. The bloke he escaped with, Taylor, got flogged as well.

'I was dirty with O'Meally when I got out and called him the Paper Tiger of Pentridge. He wanted to kill me, and it got back to him that I said he wasn't the last man to be flogged in Australia because they did Taylor second. I also told everyone that he screamed and Taylor took it like a man.'

Most of O'Meally's psychological scars were given to him during his unprecedented 11-year stay in H Division.

'It was a really shocking time,' O'Meally said. 'They inflicted some terrible punishments on people. They'll get their just deserts when they go below. You couldn't talk to anyone – or even look at anyone – without being hit by a baton. You would be batoned down for no reason what-soever; they didn't need an excuse. It seems incredible that I lasted so long down there. I saw so many take their own lives, and many more try. As I look back on those days, I don't know how I survived. I saw plenty of other men crippled, mangled, destroyed and fall by the wayside.

'I have flashbacks. Sometimes I wake up in the middle of the night and I can hear screams of blokes being belted by the screws. It was like something out of Dante's *Inferno*. The brutality was just out of this world.'

10

PEDOS, POOFTERS AND PRICKS
Cessnock, Goulburn and Risdon

Ray

The old-time Cessnock inmate proudly paraded his new pet.

'You know who this is?' he said to a fellow old-timer.

Yep.

'G'day, Ray.' The other inmate extended his right hand. 'How you finding it?'

The pet nodded. 'Yeah, no worries, mate. I'm all good here.'

The trio of men, all old enough to get a five per cent discount at IGA on Tuesdays and Thursdays, smiled as the hot summer sun rose over the yard.

'You fancy some cards, Ray?' said the first man, who was proudly showing the old man the sights: concrete yards, razor wire and the heat haze of the stinking hot Hunter Valley.

'We have a group that plays a bit every day. It's something we do to pass the time.'

Ray winked. 'I don't mind me some euchre. But I ain't got much luck when it comes to poker.'

They all laughed . . .

Raymond Reginald Williams had held a pretty good damn hand until he was forced to fold.

Anyone ever lost $5 billion?

Born in 1937, the Order of Australia medal-winner began working at the age of 13 for Guardian Insurance as a holiday filing clerk. He went on to found his first business 18 years later, a company called HIH. In 1968, Williams and Michael Payne went all out, and what started as a small partnership turned into an insurance powerhouse with about $8 billion in assets shortly before the millennium. In 1997, it was the third largest general insurer behind Australian warhorses GIO and AMP.

Then the hand turned to shit.

In 2001 the board of the company appointed liquidators, and an $800 million loss was estimated by KPMG over the six months leading to 31 December 2000.

Whoops.

The demise of HIH was the largest corporate failure in Australian financial history. Williams, who was soon stripped of his Order of Australia and had his name removed from charities and research institutions to which he had donated in excess of $20 million, stepped down as chief executive six months before liquidators were hauled in. The estimated losses totalled up to $5.3 billion.

Maybe he should have listened to Kenny Rogers's 'The Gambler'.

'One of the things I found most difficult,' Ray Williams said before charges were laid, 'was the fact that I wasn't there. Something that you nurtured from the very beginning, all those years, and just those last few months I wasn't there to help. Perhaps I would have saved it. There's no doubt you can go through many situations in the corporate world and find that things that looked impossible somehow would be saved.'

Williams blamed someone else for the collapse of his company and for the prison time he would soon serve – and that person wasn't PM John Howard, who ordered a Royal Commission into the company's collapse.

The Royal Commission handed its finding on Australia's biggest ever corporate collapse to Parliament on 16 April 2003. Justice Neville Owen, the head of the Commission, named Williams 15 times in the report, with four of the mentions being possible criminal offences.

Williams ended up with a minimum of two years and nine months. And off he went to Cessnock to play cards with a couple of old blokes . . .

The inmate giving Williams the tour, a long-time drug dealer who had seen it all, walked over to the table – black and red cards; green singlets soaked through and stinking in the summer heat.

'G'day, boys,' he said. 'Mind if we play? This is my mate, Ray.'

The inmates nodded and slid down to make room for the two old-timers.

They played a few hands. Ray was doing okay.

'All of a sudden, this young bloke got up,' said one of the card-playing inmates. 'He was a young fella from up Newcastle way. About 23 or something like that.' *Yep. Lightbulb moment.* 'Something just clicked, and he turned to Ray.'

The young inmate's eyes grew dark, stormy with suspicion.

'Ray, hey?' he said. 'What's your last name?'

Williams peered over his hand.

He had been dealt a dud.

'Williams,' he said, not shying away from who he was. 'Ray Williams, pleasure to mee–'

Crack!

Williams went crashing into the ground, the punch smashing him senseless.

The kid jumped on top and went to give him some more. 'Fuck you!' he screamed. 'You scum!'

The other old fellas intervened.

'He started laying in,' the former prisoner continued. 'And we had to pull him off.'

The kid grunted and groaned, all dishevelled, mad and looking for some more.

'We said, "You can't go bashing him, mate. He's an old man!"'

The kid attempted to break free from the card-playing codgers who were grabbing at his greens.

'Fuck that,' he screamed. 'Do you know who that prick *is*?'

Turns out the country kid, rough and tough, didn't like Ray.

'He looked at us and said, "My old nan lost her house because of him,"' the former inmate said. 'Turns out his grandmother was insured with HIH. There was a fire or something like that and her house was destroyed. Anyway, she was one of the thousands who got duded by this bloke.'

They tried to calm him down – 'He can't fight back!' – but the kid snarled and went to snap out another short right. 'Yeah,' he said, the punch only hitting air, thanks to the men pulling him back. 'Neither could me nan. Fuck him. He took her house.'

The other seniors looked at each other, shrugging their shoulders.

'He had a good point,' the former inmate said. 'But the couple he got in almost killed Ray, so we pulled him up. He couldn't take any more.'

The kid soon calmed down.

'Ray didn't have any problems after that. I think he did his time pretty easy. It was all minimum security, and I think a lot of people blamed [Rodney] Adler for what had happened . . . not Ray.'

Williams certainly blamed Adler, the former HIH director who was sentenced to four and a half years after pleading guilty to four charges relating to the collapse – according to Williams's former card-playing buddy, anyway.

'Oh yeah,' he continued. 'He used to blame Adler for all of it. He would say none of it was his fault. I mean, Ray was quite likeable. I did time with Adler too, and nobody liked that bloke because he was just a slimy prick. The only reason that no one killed him in jail is because he paid for protection. Ray didn't need to because he was in minimum and he was an old bloke. People wanted to kill Adler, but most blokes left Ray alone.

'Adler was different, and he bought every Lebo in jail a tracksuit. I was with him in Kempsey when he was paying some Islanders 500 bucks a week to look after him. They could have got a lot more out of him.'

Williams didn't do it as easy as his old buddy recalled. The disgraced businessman was moved from Cessnock to Silverwater Jail after some serious threats were made.

'A couple of blokes tried to get cash out of him,' said one Cessnock officer. 'They realised who he was, and apparently he was still loaded. Having money makes you a pretty big target in jail, and this guy was also a senior citizen.'

So the sharks circled the slow old fish.

'I think they threatened to kill him or something,' the officer continued. 'They wanted him to put a load of money in an account and said they would get him if he didn't. Anyway, we got wind of it.'

And back down the F3 he went, no doubt wishing the bus would drop him off at his multimillion-dollar North Shore home on the way. But the bus kept on going.

Eventually Williams was set free and was soon on his way back to his wife, Rita, and his double-storey home in Seaforth – *well, it was in her name of course*. Williams was released from Silverwater on 14 January 2008. The gates opened at 9am, and the 71-year-old was sent straight into another pack of circling sharks – journalists. Equally as frightening as anything he'd encountered in prison, they used questions as teeth.

Have you got a message for the people you ripped off? What do you want to say to all the people who lost their homes? Will you finally say 'sorry'?

'All I would like you to understand is that the last thing in the world I would have wanted was for HIH to fail, for people to be hurt and for people to suffer financial loss,' Williams said. 'And I really am very sorry that occurred. If I could just leave it at that, I really would like to get home and spend some time with my family, who have been so wonderfully supportive, as have our friends and even so many of the HIH staff.'

He jumped in a blue Ford Falcon and his son drove him home. He had survived . . . just.

Hey Dad – Part II

Remember the actor-turned-inmate Robert Hughes, who had a shitty reception in Goulburn? The bloke I wrote about in *Australia's Most Murderous Prison*?

Well, here's a little reminder:

The famous fish was finally here.

'Hey Dad!' the inmate yelled. 'Cop this, you kiddy-fiddling fuck!'

227

Smack! Shit slapped against Robert Hughes's face, the faecal blow forcing his cowardly eyes from the concrete and into the crowd.

'Keep walking, Hughes,' screamed a Goulburn guard, the safety of the wing sheltering him from the flying shit. 'Move!'

Hughes took another step.

Smash! A urine-filled milk carton crashed into his shoulder, stinking yellow liquid splattering his face.

'Hey Dad!' screamed another. 'Why don't you pisssssss off?'

Judge Peter Zahra predicted the 'brazen' and 'predatory' Hughes would be at 'significant risk' of harm from other prisoners when he sentenced the star of the famous Australian sitcom Hey Dad . . .! to a maximum of ten years' jail for indecently assaulting four victims, including a child co-star.

And he was right . . .

The smirk – the one Hughes wore throughout his trial, even when he was sentenced – was now gone. A carton containing faeces had slapped it from his face.

'This is Goulburn, mate,' said one of the 30 or so inmates crossing the concrete yard called 'the Circle', a section in the middle of the prison compound that connects all the jails together. 'What did you expect?'

The inmate pushed Hughes in the back. 'You walk ahead,' he continued. 'We're going to hang back a bit.'

Hughes looked to the end of the yard.

It's only 40 metres. Not that far.

Are they holding more milk cartons?

He looked to his left – inmates stood behind another fence, all tattoos, muscles and jail-yard tough.

Yep. They're milk cartons, and they're filled with shit.

Robert Hughes pissed his pants. And then he was given Goulburn Jail's shittiest-ever reception.

'They just unloaded,' recalled a Goulburn guard. 'Piss and poo – they covered him in it. It was his first day in Goulburn and he was brought out into the yard. I was standing on the Circle. Hughes was a protection inmate because of his crimes. He was never going to be put in, or out, with general population inmates because they would have killed him. But while he wasn't going into a yard with them, he had to walk through the fenced-off corridor between two other yards to get to an area called the Cookhouse before being let into the activities yard.'

The 40-metre chain-gang march from one prison block to the next was usually uneventful. But an exception was made for Hughes that afternoon; his fame and his crime made him an irresistible substitute sewer.

'I'm not sure how they knew he was coming,' the officer continued. 'But they knew. And they had all armed themselves up with shit and gone out to meet him. He was in the yellow yard, which is strict, strict protection. He was with all the rock spiders and paedophiles and was safe from them, but he wasn't safe from anything that could be thrown over or through the fence.'

The Goulburn guards did not have time to protect Hughes from the shit storm. Or maybe they just didn't want to.

'When Robert Hughes came out of that wing, I would estimate 50 to 70 inmates all ran to the yard,' the officer said. 'We thought, Oh shit, it's on here. Before we knew it, he had shit and piss thrown on him from the time he walked into the *yard to the time he walked out of the back of the yard. What they do is shit and then piss in the little milk containers they're issued, and then they put their arms through the bars and fling it. You would be really surprised how far.*

'Hughes was attacked from both sides – one was a protection yard and the other a general yard. They were all into him. The other inmates did their best to let him go first.'

Covered from head to toe in human waste, Hughes sat on top of a small grassy hill in the activities yard.

And he cried.

'He would have tried to clean himself up,' the officer said, 'but it was impossible without having a shower. He spent the entire time sitting on the hill, sooking. He was a stinking mess.'

Then he was sent back to his cell; first to the Cookhouse and then back through the yard.

'It happened again on the way back,' the officer said. 'They had reloaded and come back for more.'

Hughes held the phone against his ear.

'I can't do it,' he sobbed to his partner on the other end of the line. 'This place is horrible. I thought I would be okay, but I can't stay here. I can't stay in Goulburn. This place is hell. You have to get me out.'

A Goulburn officer overheard his conversation.

'He was crying like a baby,' the officer said. 'He was on the phone to his missus, the one who stood by him, and he was like, "I was covered in shit and piss today." It was one of the funniest phone calls ever. He had just been issued his prison greens. He was a big girl through the reception process, sobbing the whole time, begging to go back to Silverwater.'

But Hughes was not transferred, his tearful pleas falling on deaf ears. And unfortunately for Hughes – not his victims – the punishment from his prison peers continued.

'He is the only inmate in Goulburn who wears a jacket in summer,' another Goulburn officer said. 'He walks around wearing a ski jacket.'

Why?

'To stop his shirts being stained by piss,' the officer continued. 'Not just that, but spit. The inmates are more opportunistic now; they will throw whatever they have when they see him. If they have nothing, which is most often the case, then they will just spit.'

They also yell; an inmate recently split bellies with eight witty words.

'He was walking back from muster across the Circle in early February [2014], getting sent back into his wing,' revealed an officer. 'He was wearing this big fucking jacket on a 40-degree day. All was quiet and nothing was going on.

'It was one of the funniest things I can remember in the last year . . . You have to picture it. This big Aboriginal bloke broke the silence by getting up against the fence and screaming, "I'm a celebrity . . . Get me out of here!"

'The whole yard fell over laughing because they'd all been watching the reality show by the same name that had started on TV. Robert just went red, kept on walking like it wasn't meant for him.'

*

Yep . . . How could you forget Robert Hughes, the 'kiddy-fiddling fuck'?

Well, Hughesy has been busy.

Stunningly, he not only confirmed what you just read, but he attempted to use it as his *get-out-of-jail card* in an astonishing appeal.

The former *Hey Dad . . .!* star challenged his maximum ten-year sentence in the NSW Court of Criminal Appeal because he believed his trial was unfair due to 'poisonous vilification' on social media. He also claimed his sentence should be reduced because of his treatment while locked up in Goulburn Jail . . . *the pee, the poo and apparently boiling water too.*

On 25 September 2015, the court heard Hughes had been targeted by other inmates in prison despite being held in segregation.

No shit.

On the second day of his appeal, Crown Prosecutor Nicole Norman, SC, said, 'It's not challenged that a number of unfortunate incidents have happened.' Justice Monika Schmidt added, 'Including having boiling water thrown at him, which seems extraordinary in the custodial environment we're discussing.'

Hughes lost his appeal . . . but the court asked that his allegations of mistreatment be referred to the Minister of Corrective Services.

'The affidavits received from both parties raised disturbing matters as to the conditions under which the applicant is being kept in custody,' the judges found.

His lawyer, Greg Walsh, commented on the recommendation shortly after the court handed down its findings, verdict and recommendations: 'Any prisoner kept in conditions like Mr Hughes has been is a matter of real concern. He was physically assaulted on a number of occasions, and he should never have been treated that way. It's a place of punishment, prison, but it's not a place where people should be dealt with in the way that he was – in such an inhumane way.'

Well, Hughes's claims of mistreatment have not fallen on deaf ears. Yep . . . we can reveal that the 'Hey Dad . . .!' wall was built at Goulburn Jail following the referral to the Minister – a wall to stop all the poo, pee and boiling water from being hurled at Goulburn's 'shittiest' inmate.

'They actually had to bring in builders and alter the jail just because of him,' revealed a current Goulburn guard. 'Down in the Cookhouse, the place where he would get piss thrown all over him, they've put this real thick, tight wire, this special screening, which stops them from throwing shit at him. He was getting apples, oranges – whatever they could get – thrown at him.'

So were the barriers built out of decency?

'Nah,' the guard continued. 'No one here cared about it – why would we? But it went up because of his lawyer and the revelations in your last book. His lawyer kicked up a big stink and went hard at everybody. He argued for a reduced sentence because of the treatment he'd received.'

The Goulburn guards are now telling inmates armed with piss-filled cartons and shitty slingshots to think twice before they fire.

'We had to talk to the blokes who were pelting him,' the officer continued, 'and tell them to calm it down. We agreed he was a filthy mongrel, but we told them that every time they were covering him in piss they were helping him. They were helping him build a case for a sentence reduction, or at the very least helping him secure a soft placement where he would get treated like a king. We had to tell them.'

So has it stopped? *Nup.*

'It still goes on,' the officer continued. 'You can't talk sense to these young, dumb blokes, but the wall has certainly helped.'

Hughes has since launched a fresh appeal. He has applied to have his name cleared in the High Court.

Yep. I'm a celebrity . . . get me out of here.

Weird Weddings and a Whack Job

Constable Frank Weir rolled the body over, all stiff, silent and stinky.

Fuck me! No way . . .

He was staring into the dead eyes of a killer, one of Australia's most infamous inmates. A man he used to guard as a corrections officer before he quit to join the police force. A man who, not so long ago, was screaming and spitting in his face.

A sad sack of shit called Peter Schneidas: the scum who belted prison officer John Mewburn to death with a hammer in an unprovoked, sickening attack at Long Bay Jail on 10 August 1979.

What are the chances? Karma . . . Yep. Karma.

'I was working down the South Coast as a police officer,' Weir said. 'I'd worked as a corrections officer for six years before going on to do 20 years in the police force. Anyway, we got a call for a deceased in 1997. I was with another bloke, my partner at the time, and we got into the car and drove on out to The Abbey to check it out.'

The Abbey?

'Yeah, it's a convent,' Weir said. 'A place run by nuns. It's on Jamberoo Mountain Road, not far from the theme park and pretty well known down the South Coast.'

Weir went white. He looked towards his partner.

Just another body – so what?

He then looked to the nun.

'His name is Peter,' she said. 'Peter Schneidas.'

No shit.

'He was such a lovely man,' she continued. 'Came to us a while back and told us all about his terrible life. Can you believe he used to get bashed up by prison guards all the time?'

Weir bit his tongue. He wanted to tell her about the time he'd found Schneidas writing death threats to guards with poo on prison walls, but he refrained.

'I was still in shock,' Weir recalled. 'Rigor mortis had set in, and he was stiff and purple. The nun was saying he was such a lovely guy, and he had come in for reflections shortly before.'

Weir wanted to set the record straight. But how could you look at a nun in her habit and speak the horrible truth? So he looked back at the body.

'He was like an ironing board, completely lifeless,' Weir said. 'But he was undoubtedly the bloke who gave me so much trouble when I worked at Goulburn. I couldn't believe it was him. I used to look after this animal, and he comes out of jail and dies a few months later? And I'm the one who finds him dead? It had to be karma.'

Schneidas was an infamously troublesome inmate. Originally convicted for minor crimes, he – and plenty of others – claimed the prison system turned him into a killer.

Just 17 years old when he was first locked up, Schneidas was given another ten years for attacking a guard and sent to the notorious Grafton Jail to join the 'intractables'. He was deemed one of the most difficult inmates in the system and was sent to northern New South Wales to be bashed by guards, their brutality exposed in a Royal Commission.

Schneidas screamed, yelled and made a scene whenever he could. He revealed why when he became one of the first men to detail the Grafton 'reception biff'.

'I walk through the cell doors and a screw hits me across the nose with the edge of his hand,' Schneidas said of the experience. 'My nose bleeds. There are four other screws with batons. They hit me with their batons; all of them – on my knee, my back, my hands and my head. I fall. I begin to scream. I beg. I grovel. The slap of the batons on my body, the crack of my bones and my own screaming are all I can hear. I stop resisting. I can't move.

'They kick me, trying to push me along in the direction

of the wing. I try to get up. Stumbling, they kick me and I fall. They kick me again. I crawl. There's blood everywhere. They herd me with kicks and blows up the stairs. I escape into the only cell that's open. They follow me. I crawl into a corner, roll into a ball, trying to protect myself. I am afraid and screaming. Begging. They keep beating me, as if they are trying to bury me in the corner. They stop. I see shoes and trouser legs leave the cell. That is all I see. The uniforms and the batons.

'The guys in the yard laughed at me about how I responded to my reception biff. To make a noise on your reception biff was seen to be weak. I never accepted that code when being flogged. The quieter you were, the easier you made it for them. Scream and rage as loudly as you can, because if you are silent they can pretend you don't exist. They can pretend that you're a thing and not a human being. Your humanity is your voice.'

While the bashings and depravity were certainly inhumane, unjust and a bloody good reason to have a major grudge against the system, nothing can justify what Schneidas did to a 'popular', 'charming' and completely innocent officer named John Mewburn.

In protest to a looming jail transfer from Long Bay's Observation Section (OBS), he grabbed a hammer and belted the guard to death as the screw leant over to open a locked door. The relentless and sickening attack left brain matter strewn across the room.

Schneidas attempted to explain his crime, claiming he was provoked by the system.

'I am 20 years old,' he said. 'I have been through Katingal, Grafton, Maitland and OBS. I have been beaten and I have been given the reputation for violence. I have never been given a go – I have never had a decent job in jail. I admit I have hit back . . . but I have never been violent at all outside of jail, only inside in response to the way I have been treated. I have tried to behave myself in jail, but it gets me nowhere. They won't give me a chance . . . I'm not looking for trouble. I try to avoid it. I have a bad reputation and things just go from bad to worse in jail.'

No amount of 'screaming' and 'raging' could convince prison officers of his 'humanity' after he had belted Mewburn to death in a vicious protest.

'He was just a bloody animal,' Weir continued. 'I saw him playing with his own shit once. He had shat in his own hand and was using it to write names of officers on the wall of his cell. He was just one of those guys. He abused me plenty of times. He would walk up to you and start screaming in your face. And there wasn't much you could do about it because of the trouble he would cause.

'He was kept in the Goulburn High-Security Unit and was well protected. They couldn't put him in the main system because he would have been ripped to shreds.'

And boy, did he complain . . .

'He was always having a cry about something,' Weir said. 'We had 12 cells in there, six on each side, and these guys were probably the most difficult prisoners in New South Wales at the time. And he was the worst. He would whine about everything. I can remember him complaining about the starch they used in the laundry to clean his clothes. He claimed it was giving him sores and he wanted to sue.'

Another former officer who guarded Schneidas at another jail agreed that he was one of the worst inmates he ever had to deal with.

'I had him at Grafton,' said Roy Foxwell, a decorated veteran of the NSW Department of Corrective Services, now retired, who also served at Parramatta and Long Bay. 'He was already serving life when I got the displeasure of having to deal with him. He was just a bloody grub. Plain and simple. I don't know what made him that way, or why he was that way, but I can tell you he was an absolute grub of the highest order. He worked on the principle that the noisiest wheel gets the most oil. He would scream and carry on all day long.'

Yep, he would complain and demand, scream and spit into officers' faces.

'He was a manipulator at the highest order,' Foxwell said. 'But there was nothing we could do about him. He had convinced the commissioner of the day that he was a force to be reckoned with and the department was scared of him. They would give him whatever he wanted just to shut him up.'

Something he wanted – and got – was a bride. Something he didn't want – but got – was a bashing instead of a bonk after marrying Josie Grass in a maximum-security wing at Goulburn Jail.

Married? Weddings in jail?

'Oh yeah,' said an officer, who asked to remain anonymous. 'We used to do one or two a year. Back then they got married quite often. It wasn't as uncommon as it would be now. They got married in the reception area where you would have the visits. They'd do all the formalities, then the bride would go off and the groom would come back inside. It was a very strange thing.'

Even stranger when the inmate was determined to have sex.

'Schneidas wanted to consummate his marriage following the ceremony,' the officer continued. 'But he couldn't do it with Jodie because conjugal visits weren't allowed, so he decided he would do it with another inmate instead. The dirty prick decided he was going to rape someone after the wedding.'

Schneidas, sick and calculating, had already picked out his target. The guard-killer was planning on spending his honeymoon in a cell with a young boy – a recent arrival to Goulburn. He was going to rape him all night long.

Crack!

A chain clobbered Schneidas in the chin as soon as he walked into the yard.

Smack! Bang! Wallop!

The newlywed was belted black and blue. A country boy stood over him and spat in his bloodied face.

'You were going to make me your bitch, hey?' the boy screamed. 'Well, you're *my* bitch now.'

Schneidas would spend his wedding night in the hospital.

'The young fella got tipped off,' the officer continued. 'I don't know how he did it, but he got a chain and was waiting for Schneidas when he came into the yard. He flogged the shit out of him and [Schneidas] wasn't able to consummate his marriage.'

Poor Peter.

Josie Grass, an education officer, was the woman who married Schneidas while he was still serving his sentence. She began conversing with the inmate when she worked at Oxford University Press and had received letters from him requesting books.

'I have never regarded Peter as unpredictable or dangerous,' she said. 'In my view, responses, often inappropriate, were conditioned in him over years of institutionalisation in boys' homes and prisons.

'When we first met, I felt able to establish communication with him. He appeared to me to be obviously insecure with low self-esteem, the kind of façade of bombast and arrogance. But in spite of his experiences, to me anyway, he has remained gentle and kind. And this is why I became involved with him.'

Foxwell described Schneidas as a sexual fiend and prison predator. He also said Josie Grass was an 'agitator', just like him.

'He was always trying to stand over young fellas for sex. He would bribe them with dope or promise them all sorts of things he couldn't deliver. He would do whatever he could to get a head-job. He was just a filthy man. I don't think he was ever charged with a rape, but there were lots of accusations, and I'm sure plenty of them were true. The trouble is, no one wants to admit they've been raped. A bloke in Grafton complained to me that Schneidas had tried to get into his pants, but he wouldn't go through with a charge because he got threatened. And it was difficult to get a charge because it was always one word against another – there were never any witnesses or anything like that.'

But sometimes Schneidas made mistakes – young and quiet didn't always mean vulnerable and weak.

'One day he picked on the wrong bloke in Grafton,' said Foxwell. 'He was a young, raw bloke from up that way who had obviously spent a lot of time doing heavy work on a farm. Schneidas tried it on him and this bloke went *whack, whack, whack* and put him hospital. He broke his nose and possibly his jaw. We all laughed at him when he came back.'

Weir didn't laugh when he filed his report of Schneidas's death. He did, however, smile.

'We just called it in and handed it over to the coroner,' Weir said. 'We didn't investigate how he had died and, to be honest, I really don't care how he died. All I know is that he should never have been released from prison. He should have died in jail.'

The post-mortem revealed the killer had died from a heroin overdose.

Was it a hot-shot?

'Honestly,' Weir said, 'I don't think anyone cares.'

Schneidas had been released from jail ten months earlier. He was 41 when Weir rolled him over, and found the murderer dead.

Demons and Day Release

The inmate was going off.

'Get it out!' came the muffled scream through the cell door. '*Aarghhh!* Get it out now. *OUT!*'

242

The guard shrugged, fumbling with his keys as he shuffled over in the direction of the tantrum.

This is unusual. Not like Mr Anonymous at all. Don't think I've ever heard a peep out of this one . . .

The guard cracked the door.

'That, *THAT*!' the inmate pointed as he screamed, huddled in a corner. 'Get rid of it *NOW*!'

The lights came on and the officer looked, first at the hysterical prisoner in pajamas, and then at the thing of terror that was causing him to scream senselessly.

'What . . . the bed?' the officer said. 'You want me to get rid of the *bed*?'

Martin Bryant stood up and walked towards the guard, pleading with his eyes.

'Yes, the bed,' he said softly, his voice full of child-like innocence. And then he whispered, 'Get it out now, please. It's full of ghosts. It's . . . it's . . . a haunted bed. They are coming to get me. Can you get me a new one, please?'

The guard laughed. 'Yeah, good one. I hope they rip you apart, all 35 of them.'

The screw was about to shut the door, slamming the slaughtering scum in with his haunted bed and demons.

Bryant snarled and then he attacked, no longer a child but once again the murderous monster who shot 58 people in Australia's worst-ever crime: the Port Arthur Massacre.

'Porky Pig' – the cock-sucking candy-eater who you met at the start of this book – got his way. He didn't have to spend the night with his demonic doona and his spectral sheets. No, he was moved to an observation cell while awaiting his charge, his full punishment to be dished out by the boss the next day.

'It was really out of character for him,' said former senior Risdon Prison corrections officer Tony Burley. 'He wasn't an inmate who really complained about anything or really breached any prison rules or protocols. You won't hear too many stories about him being booked by prison officers.'

Except for this one . . .

'I was the one who dealt with him on this occasion,' Burley said. 'And I did have to give him some punishment. He wanted to move his bedding out of the cell because he believed it was haunted, and the officer said, "No, your bedding is your bedding, stiff shit." Bryant reacted to that and told the officer to get fucked and went at him. It wasn't a very serious matter, but a report was put in and I decided to confine him to a segregation cell for 48 hours.'

Yep, a suffocatingly small segregation cell . . . no windows, no lights.

Burley led Bryant to his punishment.

Yeah, really feel for you, mate. I do. But you can't go screaming at officers and having a go at them.

He extended his arm and ushered the mass murderer into the cell.

'It's only 48 hours,' he said. 'You'll be fine.'

Bryant nodded, agreeing with the boss.

I sure will. I showed you guys. I got rid of the damn bed.

Burley looked back at the chubby inmate who was smiling, already settling into the segregation cell.

'Oh,' Burley said, 'by the way.' He paused and pointed. 'See that bed? Well, that's *your* bed. We brought it in here from your cell. We thought we'd make you nice and comfy.'

Bang!

Burley slammed the door shut, ignoring the hysterical pleas and the fists smashing on door. He walked away, leaving Bryant all alone, in the dark, with his 35 ghosts.

'Yeah, he wasn't too happy about that,' Burley recalled. 'But that gets back to wanting to give these guys a clip over the ear at times. You can't, though, and there are better ways to deal with it. Sometimes there are different ways to get back at them.'

And this was certainly one of those times.

'Locking him down in the haunted cell with his haunted bedding?' Burley said. 'Well, he didn't give too much lip to the officers after that.'

After 48 hours in the cell with no one for company but the souls of the people he killed, Bryant was released. He was whiter than the haunted sheets.

'And he didn't say a word,' Burley said.

Out free with no guards, guns or chains, Martin Bryant was released for a walk in a public park. That is the stunning claim made by Tony Burley, the former Tasmanian prison supervisor revealing that Bryant went on day trips in November 2006.

In a startling revelation that will outrage the friends and family of those he shot, Burley said Bryant was taken out by 'unarmed' escorts during a controversial stay at the Wilfred Lopes Centre, a mental health facility for inmates with serious mental illnesses run by the Tasmanian Department of Health and Human Services.

'I was doing an investigation for an insurance company at the time, and an employee from the centre informed me he was there,' Burley said. 'It was run by the Health Department, and I was told he had been taken out on a couple of "day trips". A lot of what happened there we don't know. I actually attempted to follow them and do surveillance, but he was moved back to the main prison not long after I found out about it.'

And why had Bryant been moved to the Wilfred Lopes Centre in the first place?

Nobody really knows.

The Tasmanian government refused to even acknowledge that Bryant had been moved to the centre, let alone *why* he had been moved, until the *Tasmanian Mercury* obtained a leaked letter from Director of Prisons Graeme Barber to the state's Chief Forensic Psychiatrist Dr John Crawshaw, who'd previously gone on the record to state that the Wilfred Lopez Centre was 'definitely a hospital, a therapeutic environment'. Barber's letter read:

I direct that prisoner Martin Bryant (date of birth 7/5/67), who appears to be suffering from a mental illness, be removed from Risdon Prison complex to the Wilfred Lopes Centre, a secure mental health unit, on the following grounds.

I consider it necessary to remove the prisoner for his own health, wellbeing or safety, and for the protection of other persons. I also consider that appropriate treatment, care, rehabilitation or other services cannot be provided in the prison or its hospital, or any other institution to which the prisoner can be removed under Section 36 of the *Corrections Act 1997*.

The public was outraged. Here was the nation's worst killer being kept in a non-prison run hospital – a 35-bed unit staffed by doctors, nurses and support workers. A place where patients were not locked in and could come and go from their cells as the pleased. A facility guarded by a 3-metre fence and a private security firm.

Yep. They were up in arms. *Imagine if they knew about the mass murderer's little day trips?*

'It's just ridiculous he was ever sent there,' Burley said. 'People at the prison deemed he needed some sort of extra help and care, and they moved him to the Lopes Centre. It was out of the control of the prison service. The department had no idea what they were doing with him.'

After the leaked letters and public pummelling, Bryant was swiftly moved from the Wilfred Lopes Centre back to the brand-new $91 million Risdon Prison. He was placed in the Mersey Unit – a 'special needs' section of the prison – where he remains today.

The Tasmanian corrections department refused to comment on Bryant's alleged day release, instead passing on our queries to the Tasmanian Department of Health.

'The only reason this patient would leave the centre would be to receive necessary medical treatment,' said a health spokesman. 'And they would be accompanied by a high level of security.'

The official refused to confirm or deny if Bryant was let out as claimed. There was no suggestion by Burley that Bryant was let out for anything other than 'treatment' or that there was no security, only that the security was unarmed, and the spokesman refused to comment when this scenario was put to him.

'We call them window-lickers,' Burley said of the inmates in the Mersey Unit. 'He's not so much in segregation but in a hospital area that's separate to the rest of the prison. It's a pretty state-of-the-art place and has a health care centre, and they can keep him under constant observation. It's a unit for people on suicide watch and at risk of self-harm, and for those who don't have the cognitive skills to get through the day or in another yard without getting their throats slit.

'I remember a couple of occasions when I attended the Mersey Unit to check in on the staff, and he would be there, just staring at everyone. He would stare at all the staff and then stare at me without saying a word. I said, "What the fuck are you looking at?"

'He's that sort of a person. Not big enough to say anything, but he will stare – and that's enough to freak a lot of people out. But he'd be the least dangerous of the crazies in that unit. There are only a limited number of cells in that area,

I think about 13, and most of the other guys are far worse than him. He'd be the most well known, but he's probably the least violent and most anonymous in terms of behaviour. He's probably there for his own safety more than anything, because he's tried to kill himself a couple of times.'

No, more than just a couple . . .

In fact, Bryant had 'officially' tried to kill himself six times during his first decade behind bars, the most famous being a brazen, bloody double attempt in 2006. Despite being in an 'observation cell', where he was checked every 15 minutes, Bryant was found lying in a quickly spreading pool of blood, having slashed his neck just 48 hours after being hospitalised with slit wrists.

Prison boss Graeme Barber said the 'high-profile' inmate had used a disposable razor for the deed.

'Self-harm incidents at prisons are a regular occurrence,' he said. 'We have regular monitoring of people if they are believed to be at risk.'

And that 15-minute monitoring was the only thing that stopped Bryant from bleeding to death. *But how the hell did he get hold of a razor less than 48 hours after cutting his wrists?*

'The blade was secreted in his body,' said a prison official.

Bryant had shoved a razor up his arse in anticipation of failure before using another one to slash up his wrists. He'd successfully kept it in his clenched cheeks during a trip to Royal Hobart Hospital for 'non-life-threatening injuries'. He then pulled it out of his arse and tried to chop off his head, knowing he was being checked on every 15 minutes or less.

'He obviously hasn't been successful,' Burley said. 'And

249

a lot of them aren't. Most of the time they don't want to die, but they self-harm for attention.'

Burley was there when Martin Bryant was first sent to Risdon – not the shiny-new Risdon full of white sheets, see-through cells and spotless floors . . .

'Oh no,' he said. 'It was different back then. It was a shit jail. It was dark, cold, wet and dangerous. The conditions were so bad that prisoners could and would assault each other at will. Assaults happened every day on both inmates and officers alike. We had sieges, riots . . . the lot. It was an absolute crap prison. One of the worst in the country.'

And Bryant wasn't Porky Pig back then. No, he was still a pale, skinny murderer with long white locks and a fresh face.

'He didn't say a thing when he first came in,' Burley recalled. 'He wasn't reticent about his crime, and to my knowledge has never expressed remorse for all the people he killed. He pretty much said nothing. He sat there in silence. I can't remember much of him from back then because he was just anonymous. He would go to Hobart Hospital quite often for outpatient calls because he suffered some pretty serious burns [to his buttocks and back after setting fire to a cottage at Port Arthur]. They covered most of his body. He was obviously heavily guarded initially, but that wasn't because he was a threat to anyone – it was because of the threat the public were to him. As I said, he has never been a violent prisoner and is at the bottom of the food chain.'

Bryant was initially locked up in the prison hospital, partly for the burns he'd sustained, but mostly because everyone in the jail wanted to kill him.

'It was used to house people who were at risk of self-harm,' Burley said. 'Or those who had minor psychological problems, not necessarily psychiatric problems. We had to watch him 24 hours a day. And we had to rotate him like a pig on a spit because of the burns. He was all bandaged up, but we had to turn him all the time so his weight wasn't always on one particular burn.

'He had his own unit. He had his own shower, toilet and all the facilities he needed to be self-sufficient. It was so that he didn't have to mingle with other prisoners, so he could manage himself. There was a big fear for his safety, and he was certainly a target when he went in – he still is. But he certainly wasn't kept in segregation because of fears he would harm anyone else. He was kept in isolation for his protection and his own medical wellbeing.'

Was Burley, or the other men who guarded the monster, ever tempted to exact some jailhouse justice and give the 'self-sufficient' mass murderer a smack across the face? Or was he and the rest the guards ordered not to?

'There were no particular directives from above about how he should be treated when he was received into the prison system,' Burley said, matter-of-factly. 'He had a very high profile on the outside but little to none on the inside. He didn't rate much of a mention when it came to the prison system. I'm sure we all fought off temptation, but that's part of the job. You have to try and keep their offences out of your mind. A professional officer will not think about their offences. You can't treat a prisoner differently to any other prisoner, and you do your best to make sure they are all treated the same.'

Even Bryant? The worst killer in our nation's history?

'Well, in saying that, there are a few people who you would love to put up against the wall,' he said. 'Pin them up there and give them a double tap. Sex offenders and rapists are at the top of the list. I'm no different to any other bloke who has been in the system for 20-odd years. I have given a bloke or two a clip around the ears. And worse. But I never saw Bryant abused. I think he's someone who doesn't make our job difficult.

'Prison is a place full of criminals, and there are a lot of assaults, standovers and things happening inside and outside of the prison that makes our jobs difficult. You have to assess the danger these guys pose and, certainly, you have to be more wary of a murderer than you would be of a traffic fine offender. That's something some people have a problem with . . . But all I'm worried about is my safety and the safety of my officers when I'm walking around these people who are capable of inflicting violence and harm. You have a different set of risk management tools. The guy who ran a red light and did a runner on the cops is certainly going to require less attention than a violent murderer. Some people are just more likely to stab you in the back. Once you go through the gate you need to have a different mindset and, to be honest, you're not so worried about what they did on the outside but what they're capable of doing on the inside.'

And the only thing Bryant was capable of was sucking cock . . .
'Yeah, he was a deviant,' Burley said. 'That was his thing.'

So who was giving the chocolates to Porky Pig?

'He was locked up with some extremely violent guys,' Burley said. 'Nut jobs.'

Yep . . . complete whackos.

One of the men is Aaron Leigh Jeffery, who attacked two gorillas at Melbourne Zoo after murdering his father.

'Jeffery is probably the most dangerous man locked up in Tasmania,' Burley said. 'He actually had a punch-up with gorillas.'

Gorillas? 250kg primates? Two of them? Yep.

Jeffery, 27 at the time, caught a ferry from Tasmania to Melbourne and headed straight to the zoo, where he scaled a 5-metre enclosure and 'just went bananas' inside the zoo's Ape House. Witnesses said he was 'making monkey noises and beating his chest' after traversing the moat to attack the two fully grown gorillas, Betsy and Mzuri. Melbourne Magistrate Roger Franich ordered the quick extradition of Jeffery back to the Apple Isle to face the charges of murdering his father and going on a shooting rampage in Devonport, where he seriously wounded one man.

'He is nuts and completely dangerous,' Burley said. 'He killed his father with his bare hands before attacking the gorillas. He was a bloke who had to be moved in shackles for every escort, and he would also have to be given a calming needle in his arse. He had an afro the size of Michael Jackson's in the early days, a beard . . . all you could see were his dangerous eyes.'

Jamie Gregory McCrossen is allegedly another inmate who likes to give Bryant treats.

'Bryant has been locked up with him since day dot,' Burley said. 'He's an infamous criminal and one who is never to be released. He wrote a letter to a witness once, threatening them in his own blood. These sorts of blokes just monster Bryant and get whatever they want.'

Poetic justice delivered jailhouse style?

PRISON TALK

The following is from *The Families Handbook*, produced by the Department of Corrective Services.

BOX VISIT: Inmate is separated from visitor by a screen, and no touching is possible.

BUY-UP: Purchases made through the correctional centres.

CLASSO: Classification of inmates to varying security levels.

CORRECTIONAL CENTRE: Offical term for a prison.

COUNSELLOR: An Offender Services and Programs Officer at some centres.

DRY CELL: Bare cell where inmates are monitored, e.g. if self-harming, or if there are concerns about safety.

LOCKDOWN: All inmates are kept in their cells due to staff shortages or incident. No visits by families or external workers.

MOSP: Manager of Services and Programs.

MRRC: Metropolitan Remand and Reception Centre (Silverwater).

MUSTER: Inmate roll-call.

PAROLE: Period of the sentence that may be served in the community with conditions like reporting to a parole officer.

PRESRIBED PROPERTY: Personal items that an inmate can have.

PROHIBITED VISITOR: When a visitor is banned from visits because they have breached visiting rules.

RESTRICTED VISITOR: A visitor who has been restricted to non-contact visits. This may occur if a visitor does not follow requirements on visits.

SAPO: Services and Programs Officer.

SEGRO: Segregation – inmates are separated from other inmates for the good order and security of correctional centres.

SORC: Serious Offenders Review Council – makes recommendations about parole, classifications and programs for serious offenders.

WELFARE OFFICER: Services and Programs Officer.

The following is language used by inmates:

BONEYARD: A protection yard where 'Dogs' go to be protected.

BOOB SHOES: Prison-issued Dunlop Volleys. Velcro, not laced.

COEY: A co-offender.

CRACKING A CELL: Opening a cell.

DIRTY: Contaminated with urine. Something that has been 'pissed on'.

DOG: Someone who gives information to police.

EHR: Extreme High Risk classification.

ESCORT: Being taken out of the prison for an external appointment, which could be a court appearance, a medical appointment or a more secretive trip to meet police and inform on other prisoners.

JUNKIES: A drug addict.

JUVIE: A Juvenile Justice Centre.

KNOCKED: Killed or to be killed.

KNOCK-IN: Next in line.

KNOCK-UP: Calling a guard to a prison cell by using an intercom system.

MIN: A six-digit number (Master Index Number) assigned to each inmate, which they will carry for life.

NA: Non-Association.

NECK UP: To commit suicide, usually by way of hanging – to 'neck yourself up' – and mostly done with sheets. It's the reason shoelaces are banned in prisons.

OBS CELL: Observation cell that can be easily seen into and is usually where the 'spinners' are held.

ONE OUT, TWO OUT and FOUR OUT: The number of men who live in a cell.

ON THE NOD (MURRAY COD): Heavily affected by drugs.

PROTECTION: Asking to be put in a yard separate from the general population because of fears for your safety.

RAMP or RAID: A cell search.

ROCK SPIDER, PEDO, KIDDY-FIDDLER: A man who has been convicted of sexually assaulting a child.

SCREW, CHIEF, BOSS and GUARD: A corrections officer.

SHIV: A weapon made from materials found inside the prison.

SPINNER (BAKED DINNER): A person with a mental problem.

SWEEPER: An inmate given the responsibility of running a jail wing.

SELECT BIBLIOGRAPHY

Aubusson, K.; Levy, M. and Pearson, A.; 'Goulburn jail escapee Beau Wiles arrested and charged', *Sydney Morning Herald*, 2 October 2015

Connolly, E., 'Hijacked driver was warned of kneecapping', *Sydney Morning Herald*, 24 February 2001

Corrective Services NSW, 'Fact Sheet: mobile phone jamming trial at Lithgow Correctional Centre', undated, 2015

Dale, A., 'A slap from behind bars: prisoner ordered beatings', *Daily Telegraph*, 27 July 2011

Dale, J., 'Rope and glory', *Sun-Herald*, 10 March 2002

Duncan, P., 'Bryant return to jail', *Tasmanian Mercury*, 30 November 2006

G, T., 'H was for Hell Division', *Herald Sun*, 3 September 1994

Hall, L., 'Accused murderer Tony Halloun admits inventing story about armed robbery', *Sydney Morning Herald*, 9 September 2014

Hall, L., 'Drugs, high society, gangster dreams', *Sydney Morning Herald*, 11 May 2011

Hall, L., 'Tradesman Tony Halloun jailed for murder of doctor's wife', *Sydney Morning Herald*, 5 December 2014

Harris, L. and McClellan, B., 'ISIS supporter put former Australian soldier in critical condition in prison assault', *Daily Telegraph*, 10 April 2016

Hazzard, B., 'Banned band jammed: jail trial extended', Minister for Justice Media Release, 9 July 2014

Inman, M., 'Spike in phone seizures at Canberra jail', *Canberra Times*, 6 April 2015

Justice Action, 'Supermax's cruel and degrading conditions', www.justiceaction.org.au, undated

Kennedy, L., 'Joy flight that visited maximum security', *Sydney Morning Herald*, 26 March 1999

Kennedy, L., 'Jailbreak duo caught in cabin 14', *Sydney Morning Herald*, 10 May 1999

Killick, J., *Gambling for Love*, Connor Court Publishing Ltd, 2015

Korn, N., 'A Vicious Life', *Sydney Morning Herald*, 10 February 1999

McClellan, B. and Benns, M., 'He unmade his bed now escapee must lie in it', *Daily Telegraph*, 20 August 2015

McClellan, B., 'The Shure-Shag Redemption', *Daily Telegraph*, 1 October 2015

Matthews, B., *Intractable: Hell Has a Name, Katingal: Life Inside Australia's First Super-max Prison*, Pan Macmillan, Sydney, 2006

Morton, J., *Maximum Security: The Inside Story of Australia's Toughest Gaols'*, Pan Macmillan, Sydney, 2011

Neales, S., 'Why Bryant was moved', *Tasmanian Mercury*, 27 November 2006

Olding, R., '$300 for a pack of cigarettes', *Sydney Morning Herald*, 16 October, 2015

O'Neil, M., 'Ready for Revenge', *Sunday Telegraph*, 27 September 2009

Osbourne, D., *Pentridge: Behind the Bluestone Walls*, Echo, 2015

Rattenbury, S., 'Inquiry into referred 2014-15 Annual and Financial Reports', Legislative Assembly for the ACT, 13 and 20 November 2015

Severin, P., 'Body orifice scanner for Goulburn prison', Corrective Services NSW Press Release, 8 Jan 2016

About the Author

James Phelps is an award-winning senior reporter for the *Daily* and *Sunday Telegraph* in Sydney. He began as an overnight police rounds reporter before moving into sport, where he became one of Australia's best news-breaking rugby league reporters.

James became News Australia's Chief National Motorsports writer and travelled the world chasing F1 stories, as well as becoming Australia's No. 1 V8 Supercar reporter. James is also a senior feature writer for the *Sunday Telegraph*.

Following the bestselling *Dick Johnson: The Autobiography of a True-Blue Aussie Sporting Legend*, James returned to his roots to delve into the criminal underworld with *Australia's Hardest Prison: Inside the Walls of Long Bay Jail*; *Australia's Most Murderous Prison: Behind the Walls of Goulburn Jail*; *Australia's Toughest Prisons: Inmates* and *Green Is the New Black*. James is a twice V8 Supercar media award-winner and a former News Awards 'Young Journalist of the Year' and 'Sport Reporter of the Year', as well as a Kennedy Awards finalist for 'Sports Reporter of the Year'.

Green Is the New Black

Ever wondered what life is like for our Aussie jailbirds?
Is it as bad as *Wentworth* or *Orange is the New Black*?
No. It's worse.

Ivan Milat, the notorious backpacker serial killer, is not the most feared person in the prison system. Nor is it Martin Bryant, the man responsible for claiming 35 lives in the Port Arthur massacre. No, the person in Australia controversially ruled 'too dangerous to be released', the one who needs chains, leather restraints and a full-time posse of guards is Rebecca Butterfield: a self-mutilating murderer, infamous for slicing guards and stabbing another inmate 33 times.

But Butterfield is not alone. There's cannibal killer Katherine Knight, jilted man-murderer Kathy Yeo, jailbreak artist Lucy Dudko, and a host of others who will greet you inside the gates of Australia's hardest women's jails. You will meet drug dealers, rapists and fallen celebrities. You will hear tales of forbidden love, drug parties gone wrong and guards who trade 40-cent phone calls for sex.

All will be revealed in *Green Is the New Black*, a comprehensive account of women's prison life by award-winning author and journalist James Phelps.